VEGETARIANISM
and the
JEWISH TRADITION

VEGETARIANISM
and the
JEWISH TRADITION

by
LOUIS A. BERMAN

KTAV PUBLISHING HOUSE, INC.
NEW YORK

Library of Congress Cataloging in Publication Data

Berman, Louis Arthur
  Vegetarianism and the Jewish tradition.

  Bibliography: p.
  Includes index.
  1. Vegetarianism—Moral and religious aspects—
Judaism.   2. Ethics, Jewish.   I. Title.
TX392.B44   296.7   81-11729
ISBN 0-87068-756-5   AACR2
ISBN 0-87068-285-7(pbk.)

Portraits on the front cover are arranged in alpha-
betical order. Top row *(left to right)*—S. Y. Agnon
(photo copyright Alfred Bernheim), A. D. Gordon,
Franz Kafka, Rabbi Abraham Isaac Kook. Bottom
row—Reverend Chaim Maccoby, Miss Vivien Pick,
Isaac Bashevis Singer, Jonathan Wolf. To locate comments on each of the above persons in this volume, see
General Index.

Manufactured in the United States of America

Dedicated to William Cumming Rose, Professor Emeritus of Biochemistry at the University of Illinois at Urbana, whose discovery of the essential amino acids replaced the risk and guesswork of vegetarian practice with reliable knowledge. His discovery has become a guiding principle of scientific vegetarianism, and merits Professor Rose the traditional Hebrew blessing—

בָּרוּךְ אַתָּה, יְיָ אֱלֹהֵינוּ, מֶלֶךְ הָעוֹלָם, שֶׁנָּתַן מֵחָכְמָתוֹ לְבָשָׂר וָדָם.

Blessed art Thou, O Lord our God, King of the universe, who has given from His wisdom to flesh and blood.

CONTENTS

PREFACE AND ACKNOWLEDGMENTS

Vegetarianism came into my life around 1973, when my son, Daniel, then a teen-ager, quietly announced that he had decided to eat no more meat. As a parent and an academic man, I went to the library shelves for reassurance that my son's decision was not too risky, and for guidance in planning a healthful food regimen for him. Searching through lists of organizations I could write to for information, I discovered that there existed in London a Jewish Vegetarian Society. I joined and began to receive their quarterly bulletin, the *Jewish Vegetarian*, which stimulated my thinking along lines which eventually produced this book.

Originally I wanted to produce a psychological study titled something like "The Religious Values of Vegetarians," while on sabbatical leave. To prepare a research proposal, I read all I could on the topic, and designed an interview study comparing vegetarian and nonvegetarian siblings. Research money for my project seemed impossible to get, so I continued my background reading until I had enough ideas to start a book on the spiritual aspect of vegetarianism. As a Jew, my thinking and writing on the topic draws upon the Jewish tradition—relating vegetarianism to the biblical emphasis on compassion for animals, to the riddle of Temple sacrifice, and to the Jewish dietary laws. My background in Jewish studies is good enough to formulate hypotheses but too limited to pursue them, so I called upon and received generous help from able scholars. I was particularly fortunate to prevail upon Dean Nathaniel Stampfer, of the Spertus College of Judaica, to translate for me Rabbi Abraham Isaac Kook's essay, "A Vision of Peace and Vegetarianism."

On the secular side, I studied the evidence of paleoanthropology concerning man's early food habits. I developed a familiarity with the biochemistry of the amino acids and with man's nutritional needs. I thought about the psychological roots of human compassion, which psychologists of a generation ago called *altruism* and present-day scholars have dubbed *pro-social behavior*.

As I embarked upon this wide-ranging study, vegetarianism found a place not only in my intellectual interests but likewise in my eating habits! First I shared my son's vegetarian meals, and gradually I became a vegetarian more or less completely. When my son left home to continue his college studies, I continued to experiment with vegetarian cookery—making dishes that were easy, nutritious, and low in cholesterol. When people learned that I was a vegetarian, they would ask questions. They would want recipes. I thought of adding an Appendix to my book, containing my favorite recipes and the results of my kitchen experimentation.

Writing a book is in many ways a solitary and lonely task. A Jewish proverb says, "A person can eat alone but he cannot work alone." How true! My efforts have been buoyed up by the help, guidance, and expressions of interest offered by many people and groups. My thoughts were sharpened by attentive and challenging audiences I addressed at Congregation Rodef Shalom in Denver, Temple Emanuel in Beverly Hills, Temple Israel in Dayton, the Downtown Synagogue in Chicago, the University of Chicago Hillel House, the Hillel group at my own campus, the University of Illinois at Chicago Circle, the Jewish Reconstructionist Congregation in Evanston, and the Third Unitarian Church of Chicago.

I have been stimulated by those who expressed an ongoing interest in my topic—including Mr. Ben Fain, of the Jewish Book Mart in Chicago, Rabbi Joseph B. Glaser, Executive Secretary of the Central Conference of American Rabbis, and Rabbi David Polish, of Beth Emet, in Evanston.

Among those whose expertise was of great help to me was Rabbi Nathaniel Stampfer, whom I have already mentioned, Rabbi Jacob Milgrom, Professor of Near Eastern Studies at the University of California at Berkeley, Professor Charles Warren of the Anthropology Department at Chicago Circle, Mr. Philip Pick, President of the Jewish Vegetarian Society, and my Yiddish translator, Mr. Jack Weinman, of the Anshe Emet Day School in Chicago. My Evanston neighbor and fellow vegetarian Lori

Lippitz offered valuable suggestions on both the form and content of my writing. My dear friend and colleague at the Circle, Professor Laurette Kirstein, read and commented upon various portions of the book. Mr. Robert J. Milch, whom my publisher chose to edit the manuscript, brought to the task an admirable range of knowledge and a master-editor's touch. Whatever merits the reader finds in this book are the results of this generous assistance.

L.A.B.

University of Illinois
at Chicago Circle
August 28, 1980

FOREWORD

by
Rabbi Zalman Schachter

In this book Dr. Louis Berman maintains that vegetarianism can draw much inspiration and support from the Hebrew Bible and from rabbinical thought. I would like to endorse his thesis.

When food-conscious people wring their hands about the burdensome costs of modern technology, frequently the topic is pollution, harmful additives, or over-refined foods. I would like to point to two other unwanted side-effects of modern technology, and show how vegetarianism counteracts them.

Large-scale agriculture, modern transportation, and food processing make it possible to eat the same foods all year 'round, thus blurring our awareness of the changing seasons. Awareness of the passage of time is an important aspect of Jewish life. Pesach begins on the night of the full moon of the vernal equinox. Succoth begins on the night of the full moon of the autumnal equinox. Our sages speak of summer foods and winter foods. The *karpas* of Pesach and the *tsimmis* of *Rosh Ha'shana* symbolize the time of the year as well as the theme of the holiday. Professor Heschel put it beautifully when he said that as Jews we live more in time than we live in space. In today's world, a vegetarian keeps in closer touch with the cycle of seasons than a meat-eater.

Modern life separates man not only from the seasons of the year, but from the sick (who are sent off to medical centers), from the old (who are hidden away in nursing homes), from the mentally incompetent (who are likewise "put away"), and also from the suffering of slaughtered animals, which is now likely to occur thousands of miles away from where a chicken or a pound of hamburger is purchased at the supermarket, pre-wrapped in the same clear plastic and white tray as an eggplant or bunch of broccoli. When our grandmother brought a live chicken to the *shochet*, she witnessed a sacred and skillful act intended to minimize the distress that is felt by both the victim and the meat-eater when an animal is killed for food. By direct observation she was thus qualified to transmit to her family the sentiment that, unlike everything else on the table, animal food comes to a Jewish table as a special dispensation and through the hands of a person dedicated to the service of God.

Today a kosher poultry-processing plant may hire, perhaps, a hundred *shochtim*. Not one customer ever sees their ceremonial acts or functional skills. The screeching, squawking chickens are herded into the plant, and leave as frozen "food products," attractively wrapped in plastic bags for display at supermarket counters throughout the country. The ranks of vegetarians might be swelled considerably if one had to watch a creature being killed before one could eat of its flesh.

In earlier days it was the prerogative of any normal adult who raised his own animals to slaughter them according to the laws of *shechita*. For the paschal sacrifice, one could slaughter a lamb from his own flock. These experiences gave one an immediate knowledge of the fact of death which transforms living creatures into food. A woman was as well-qualified as a man, in principle, if not in physical strength, to perform the acts of *shechita*. (Among the Jews of Italy, this question arose several hundred years ago when men stayed in the cities while their families vacationed in the Alps. Rabbi Chaim Yosef Azulai of Livorno wrote a responsum stating that women did indeed have the right to perform *shechita*.)

Our forefathers were a pastoral people. Raising animals for food was their way of life. Not only did they eat meat, they drank water and wine from leather flasks, they lived in tents and wore clothes made from skins and sewed together with bones and sinews. They read from a Torah written on parchment, used a ram's horn as a *shofar*, and said their morning prayers with leather *tefillin*. Not surprisingly, the Temple worship of this pastoral people included offerings of their best animals to God. Perhaps the best defense of this ritual is that it replaced human sacrifice, as the story of

the binding of Isaac so clearly suggests. Agricultural offerings (vegetarian offerings!) also had their place on the Temple altar—*terumah, challah,* flour
mixed with oil, and wine.

How remarkable that a pastoral people should give the world a vision
of a time of Creation when there was no eating of meat, and of a time of
the Messiah when "the lion will eat straw like the ox" (when all the world
would be vegetarian?). The compassion with which a shepherd was ex-
pected to treat his animals was implied in the description of God as a
shepherd ("The lord is my shepherd . . . ") and as One whose mercies ex-
tend to all His creatures.

Clearly, our forefathers were not only meat consumers; as a pastoral
people they were also meat-producers. Does this fact make the practice of
vegetarianism a stain upon the memory of our forefathers? Some well-
meaning people apparently think so, and I recall with deep regret once
reading a *teshuvah* by a young *possek* opposing vegetarianism as a Jewish op-
tion. Our forefathers also practiced polygamy. Are we ashamed to recall
that Abraham had two wives because in today's Western world he would
be called a bigamist? Vegetarianism is a response to *today's* world—medical,
scientific, economic. Meat-eating, like polygamy, fit into an earlier stage of
human history. Unlike polygamy, meat-eating is still the dominant practice
in the world around us, but vegetarianism is surely a foretaste of life on
earth in generations ahead.

The adoption of vegetarianism does not imply that all other food
customs are "bad," any more than adherence to monogamy makes
polygamy "bad." In Jewish thought, the world is too complex and subtle
to compartmentalize and label sacred and profane, mundane and spiritual,
good and bad. A Talmudic midrash goes: "Let not a man say, 'I do not like
the flesh of swine.' On the contrary, he should say, 'I like it but must abstain, seeing that the *Torah* has forbidden it.' " (*Sifre* 11-22).

The traditionalist argues that in Jewish life the eating of meat is not
only permitted, it is regarded as a *mitzvah.* One *must* celebrate the Sabbath
with the eating of fish, fowl, and meat. I recall the thought of Rabbi Israel
Salanter, that the sages set down this rule for the benefit of the poor, who
depended upon the *kupat ha'kahal* to appease their hunger. Thus were the
administrators of *zedakah* obliged to provide the needy with what was considered substantial food, at least once a week.

There were always Hasidim who tasted meat only on Sabbath and holidays, and at all other times abstained from meat-eating because, they claimed, they were not in the proper state of consciousness to eat in the manner of Temple priests. Only on the Sabbath—when "the righteous eat to satisfy the soul" (Proverbs 13:35)—do they permit themselves the eating of meat.

Vegetarian practices occur elsewhere in traditional life. Many *ba'ale teshuvah*, penitents, abstain from eating anything that comes from a living creature, and this includes milk, cheese, and eggs, as well as meat. So too it was the custom of Rav Kook's disciple Nazir not to eat of anything that came of a living creature.

The Laws of Moses called upon the Hebrew tribes to become a holy people, and therefore to eat only what befits a holy people; not to defile their bodies, as one would not defile a Temple. Christianity rejected the Mosaic laws with the words that what is important is not what goes into the mouth but what comes out of it. But, alas, we have lived to see the day when both the scientific community and the public at large are indeed concerned about what goes into the mouth—tobacco smoke that may cause cancer of the lungs, over-refined foods that may lead to cancer of the colon, growth-accelerators that may cause cancer in other parts of the body. We now read the words of Leviticus with a new consciousness: "Be ye a holy people. Do not defile yourself."

There is a painful incongruity in the idea of a halakhic authority inhaling deeply on a cigarette as he ponders a question of *kashrut*. Can a substance at the same time be kosher and dangerous to health? This is a question that will not go away, a question that asks our scholars to get in touch with the new consciousness about food and health.

This gap between our religious community and the new food-awareness is illustrated to me by the experience of a young man who became a *ba'al teshuvah* and moved into a traditional Jewish neighborhood to make it easier for him to observe the *kashrut* laws. He complained to me that in his adopted surroundings there were no natural food stores, and there was less interest in matters of nutrition—virtually no concern about the overconsumption of refined sugar and flour, eggs, and saturated fats. There even seemed to be less awareness of what it means to eat from the yield of nature. He asked, "Why can't Torah help me reach a high level of food consciousness?"

Surely Torah does support the interest of many young people of today in nutrition in general, and in vegetarianism in particular. That, I think, is the author's thesis, and I invite you to judge how well he has carried out his task.

Temple University
Philadelphia, Pa.
November 20, 1980

INTRODUCTORY REMARKS ON VEGETARIANISM

by
Dr. Jean Mayer

What is vegetarianism? . . . The ideal diet, adopted by the perfect man in the Garden of Eden and destined to return with the coming of the Messiah? Or may vegetarianism also be a practical and nutritionally sound food practice for ordinary people, imperfect though normal, today? If this question is on your mind as you open this book, you are entitled to an answer right away. The answer you want cannot come from a vegetarian enthusiast or from a professor of psychology who became interested in vegetarianism and the Jewish tradition. But perhaps you *would* like to know what has been said about vegetarianism by a professor of nutrition at a leading American university.

To satisfy the interested but skeptical reader who first wants an expert outside opinion on vegetarian practice, here is an extract from *A Diet for Living*, by Dr. Jean Mayer,* a nutrition guidebook adopted by Consumer's Union for distribution to its members.

---

*Who is America's foremost authority on nutrition? A strong candidate for this title would be Dr. Jean Mayer, formerly Professor of Nutrition in the School of Public Health, Harvard University, and currently President of Tufts University, Medford, Massachusetts. Dr. Mayer served as Chairman of the Committee on Food, Nutrition, and Health of the President's Consumer Advisory Council. His writings have appeared in technical journals and in general publications. "On Nutrition," his syndicated column, appears in newspapers throughout the United States.

Dr. Mayer was born in France, and earned a D.Sc. in physiology, *summa cum laude*, at the Sorbonne. During World War II he served in both the French Army and the Free French Forces and was awarded fourteen decorations, including the *Croix de Guerre*. After the war, he studied at Yale University, and earned a Ph.D. in physiological chemistry.

The author's correspondence with Dr. Mayer evoked the following comment from Dr. Mayer: "The relationship of vegetarianism to religion and the ethical treatment of animals is a subject that interests me very much." This attitude shines through Dr. Mayer's references to vegetarianism in his books and articles. The above quotation from *A Diet for Living* (pp. 183–184) is used with Dr. Mayer's permission.

My son came home from school, and as he sat at the dinner table, he cast a disdainful eye on the roast and announced he had become a vegetarian. What could have brought this about?

His motivation may be compassion (why should we kill other animals to feed ourselves?) or it may be imaginary health reasons (meat causes cancer). Or it could be an Oriental philosophy (the Zen Buddhist way of eating is necessary for longevity and rejuvenation).

We told the boy to stop being ridiculous and to eat his meat. He responded by declaring that only insensitive persons endowed with the grossest type of sensuality would eat meat. All he wanted was some rice or nuts or beans. Isn't there anything we can do to change his attitude?

The direct order, which you unsuccessfully tried, is likely to be, in contemporary jargon, counterproductive. It might be more useful if you or your husband were to conduct a calm, interested conversation after the meal to determine how far the young man plans to deviate from the normal eating patern, and why.

The danger to the youngster—and thus the extent of the need for parental intervention—varies enormously. It depends on whether he has become a convinced but sensible vegetarian who mildly limits his diet or whether he has fallen for the truly hazardous extremes of the Zen macrobiotic diet. . . .

Quite often the young person is horrified at innocent animals being driven to the slaughterhouse to satisfy the appetites of the human species which could easily feed itself in other ways. Most vegetarians animated by such convictions are in no way averse to drinking milk or to eating nonfertile eggs. They are classified as "ovo-lacto-vegetarians."

Are there nutrients lacking in the diets of these people?

As far as we know, this type of diet provides perfectly satisfactory nutrition. With plenty of milk and cheese and eggs every day, meat will in no way be missed. Protein, calcium, B_2, iron and trace minerals will be present in quite sufficient amounts in the diet. Exhaustive studies of Seventh-Day Adventists who are ovo-lacto-vegetarians, have repeatedly shown them to be in excellent health.

But what if our son has embraced complete vegetarianism?
If he refuses any animal food whatsoever, there may be problems. As long as he is ready to have a varied vegetarian diet—with beans, nuts, whole-grain cereals and plenty of fruits and vegetables—the most serious risk is not, as you might think, lack of protein. The real problem is Vitamin B_{12} deficiency. In the long run, if allowed to go uncorrected, it portends a severe danger. . .

If your child persists in following such a diet, try to get him to compromise by eating nonfertile eggs or at least (like Gandhi) milk and cheese. If you cannot negotiate this arrangement, he must have a daily vitamin pill containing vitamin B_{12}.

1

One Man's Meat Is
Another Man's Porridge

In Genesis, the words of God are given as: "Behold, I have given you every herb yielding seed, which is upon the face of all the earth, and every tree, in which is the fruit of a tree yielding seed—to you it shall be for food."[1] The King James Version reads: "to you it shall be for *meat*" (emphasis added). A look at the Hebrew text gives the original word as *akhlah*, "food." How did the word *meat* come into the King James Version?

Simply put, in the time of King James, and to a lesser extent today, *meat* may be defined as "food in general, solid food in contradistinction to drink." That is the first definition of *meat* listed in the *Oxford English Dictionary* (OED), although to that definition is appended the warning that this meaning of the word is now archaic and dialectal. OED lists the following citations from English literature in which the word *meat* is used in this older sense:

Thy mete shall be mylk, honye, & wyne. (1477)

Our guides told us that the horses could not travel all day without rest or meat. (1794)

Meat is set down to them on a flat plate, consisting of crumbled bread and oatmeal. (1893)

As early as 1460, animal flesh was referred to as *butcher's meat* or *butcher-meat*. What are now called *baked goods* were once called *bake-meat*.

Articles of food prepared from milk were called *milk-meat* or *white-meat*. In modern English, *sweetmeat* and *nutmeat* refer to food which has no animal origin at all.

It looks as if the word *meat* came to be adopted as a euphemism for animal flesh. The words *beef, pork, veal, poultry,* and *game* are themselves euphemisms for the flesh of a cow, pig, calf, chicken, and wild animal. *White meat* and *dark meat* sound less anatomical than *breast* and *thigh*. Blood and fat become more appetizing when the mixture is referred to as *natural gravy* or *drippings*. In England, a kind of sausage made of blood and suet is known euphemistically as *black pudding*.

An appealing label helps cope with a food taboo. In Iran, when a cook prepared ham or bacon for a European, he referred to it as *nightingale's flesh*.[2] Many Chinese Moslems will eat pork freely "if it is called *mutton* or some other name."[3] In present-day Israel, a nonobservant Jew may refer to pork as *white meat*.

The popularity of euphemisms for animal flesh suggests that perhaps humans have mixed feelings about using flesh as food. Is this bias a vestige of the Bible's emphasis on compassion for animals, or is this attitude too widespread to be ascribed to the Hebrew Bible? Is compassion for animals a mark of high civilization, or do we see it among tribal peoples? First, let us ask how far the Hebrew Bible goes in advocating compassion for animals, and how these commandments have been interpreted in the post-Biblical texts.

2

Compassion for Animals in the Hebrew Bible

It is not enough to say that kindness to animals is mentioned in the Hebrew Bible. The fact that the welfare of animals is mentioned in the Ten Commandments and that compassion toward animals is the topic of passages in a number of books of the Bible, justifies the statement that compassion toward animals is an important theme of the Hebrew Bible.

The Fourth Commandment designates the Sabbath as a day of rest for man and his work animals alike. "Observe the Sabbath day. . . . In it thou shalt not do any manner of work, thou, nor thy son, nor thy daughter . . . nor thy cattle, nor thy stranger that is within thy gates . . . "[1]

The Sabbath is not the only day on which animals are to be shown consideration. In Deuteronomy, concern is likewise expressed about the day-to-day treatment of domestic animals. "Thou shalt not plow with an ox and ass together."[2] "Thou shalt not muzzle the ox when he treadeth out the corn."[3] The Code of Jewish Law holds that if this commandment is to be carried out in spirit, it follows that:

1. The rule applies not only to oxen, but to all beasts, clean or unclean.
2. The rule applies not only to corn, but to all products. Only if the product is injurious to the animal is it permissible to muzzle.
3. If the beast cannot eat through being thirsty, give it to drink.
4. Even if the beast belongs to a heathen, if it is muzzled, the Israelite transgresses the law.
5. An Israelite is forbidden to muzzle a beast by shouting at it to prevent it from eating.[4]

Farmers may demand more obedience from their human helpers than from their work animals, said the rabbis. Men "may be forbidden to consume that which they harvest, but animals must be allowed to feed if they so desire, for while men can understand deprivation, animals cannot."[5]

In Deuteronomy, compassion toward animals is again the theme of the commandment that if one sees a fallen ox or ass, one must help the owner lift the animal up again.[6] And again, it is commanded not to disturb a mother-bird in her nest with her eggs or young.[7] Maimonides commented that if the Torah provides that animals and birds should not be caused grief, "how much more careful must we be that we should not cause grief to our fellow men."[8]

In the Book of Proverbs, man is asked to treat animals with compassion, as God is merciful to all his creatures. "A righteous man regardeth the life of his beast."[9] In the Book of Psalms, praise is expressed to a God who is merciful to man and beast --

Thy mercy, O Lord, is in the heavens; and thy faithfulness reacheth unto the clouds.

Thy righteousness is like the great mountain; thy judgments are a great deep; O Lord, thou preservest man and beast.[10]

In the Book of Exodus the law is given that "if an ox gore a man or a woman [and] they die, the ox shall be surely stoned."[11] Erich Isaac sees this law as meaning that animals not only have rights (e.g., the right to Sabbath rest, and the right to protection against needless suffering), but they also have responsibilities. From a Biblical point of view, says Isaac, the gap between human and animal life seems very small indeed.

In the Book of Numbers appears the familiar story of Balaam, the pagan soothsayer dispatched by the Moabites and Midianites to visit and lay a curse upon the Hebrews. God sends an angel to stop Balaam, and the ass upon which the soothsayer is riding at once sees an "angel of the Lord standing in his way." The animal turns away from the path, then crushes Balaam's foot against a wall, and finally lies down under his rider. Each time, Balaam is angry and confused, smites his ass, and finally "the Lord opened the mouth of the ass and said unto Balaam: 'What have I done unto thee? . . . Am I not thine ass, upon which thou hast ridden all thy life long unto this day? Was I ever wont to do this unto thee?' And he said:

'Nay.' Then the Lord opened the eyes of Balaam, and he saw the angel of the Lord standing in the way . . . and he bowed his head and fell on his face. And the angel of the Lord said unto him: 'Wherefore hast thou smitten thine ass these three times? [I have come to save you from your own destruction] and the ass saw me, and turned aside from me, surely now I had even slain thee, and saved her alive.' And Balaam said unto the angel of the Lord: 'I have sinned; for I knew not that thou stoodest in the way against me.''[12]

Maimonides quotes from this passage ("Wherefore hast thou smitten thine ass?") as a basis for the "rule laid down by our Sages, that it is directly prohibited in the Torah to cause pain to an animal . . . "[13]

Over the centuries, the rabbis have been divided over whether the ass actually uttered words or whether he gave a wild cry which Balaam *understood* as a protest against the cruel beatings.[14] This interpretation would suggest that the utterances of animals not only express feelings but also convey messages. The story also suggests that at a given moment an animal may be more sensitive than a human to God's will.

The Code of Jewish Law contains several sections on the protection of animals—sparing them from burdensome or annoying labor, assuring them of rest on the Sabbath, providing them with sufficient food, alleviating their suffering even if it occurs on the Sabbath.[15] The following quotations are representative:

It is forbidden, according to the Torah, to hurt any living creature. It is, on the contrary, one's duty to save any living creature be he ownerless or if it belong to a non-Jew.

When horses which are drawing . . . a cart come to a rough place or to a high hill and they cannot draw the cart without help, it is a religious duty to help even the horses of a non-Jew, because of the precept forbidding cruelty to animals, lest the owner smite them to make them draw more than their strength permits.[16]

Erich Isaac notes that the Bibical command to spare animals from suffering also led the rabbis to elaborate the following rules about work animals:

A person may charge for loading an animal but not for unloading it.

"If a person is asked to help in loading and in unloading by different parties, he must first unload because it is the already burdened animal which needs relief.[17]

In addition to the practical ministration to the well-being of animals, the Laws of Moses specify several symbolic expressions of compassion. "Thou shalt not seethe a kid in his mother's milk"[18]—the law that has generated so many details of *kashruth*. A similar regard for the mother-offspring relationship is contained in the law that neither a cow and its own calf nor a ewe and its own lamb should be killed on the same day.[19] Rabbi J. H. Hertz interprets this law as an effort to reduce the likelihood that a young animal be slain in the sight of its own mother. Rabbi Hertz notes the judgment of Maimonides that man and animals differ in the capacity for reason but that the capacity for feeling "exists not only in man but in most living things." Therefore it must be supposed that the sight of its own offspring being slaughtered must cause a mother-animal enormous grief.[20]

In the Responsa literature, hunting is deplored as wasteful, unnecessarily cruel, and dangerous to human life.[21] In the Code of Jewish Law, no special blessing is given for meat dishes. "It is not fitting to bless God over something which He created and which man has slain."[22] It is also forbidden to celebrate the acquisition of a leather garment.

It is customary to bless someone who acquires a new garment—Mayest thou wear out this garment and acquire a new one. This blessing should not be said, however, for leather shoes, or for a garment made of leather, even if the leather parts are not visible, because to acquire a new garment like this one requires the killing of a living being, and it is written: " . . . His mercy is upon all His works.[23]

It is a custom not to wear leather shoes on Yom Kippur. One does not ask forgiveness of his sins while wearing articles made from the skins of slaughtered animals.[24]

What is the moral message underlying this Bibical emphasis on kindness to animals? We have already mentioned Maimonides' comment that if the Torah protects birds and animals from grief, "how much more careful must we be that we should not cause grief to our fellow men."[25] On this note, Rabbi Hertz writes that the theme of compassion for animals is of profound importance for the humanizing of man.[26]

Another implication, writes Rabbi Hertz, is that there is an unbroken continuity in the scale of all living creatures. Life is life, whether it is an animal's or a human's.[27] Rabbi Harry Cohen asserts that before the Hebrew Bible there was no code of law which protected animals as well as human beings.[28] Neither the Koran nor the New Testament, he adds, explicitly *commands* kindness to animals.[29]

By way of contrasting the regard for animal life in the Hebrew Bible with the New Testament, Rabbi Hertz observes Paul's argument that the Mosaic law against muzzling a threshing ox must symbolize something that concerns humans, not animals. "Doth God take care for oxen?" Paul asks rhetorically. "Or saith he it altogether for our sakes? For our sakes, no doubt," he argues.[30] Peter compares evildoers to "natural brute beasts, made to be taken and destroyed."[31]

If it is fair to say that the central theme of the Hebrew Bible is the preservation and enhancement of life, and the central theme of the New Testament is the glorification of the soul, then it must be noted that life is something that man and animals do have in common—but the soul, by definition, is a peculiarly human possession.[32] It is therefore not surprising that a greater kinship between man and animals is expressed in the Hebrew Bible than in the New Testament.

If compassion toward animals is such an important Biblical theme, why is it permitted that animals be slaughtered and eaten? This is a question which the sages have attempted to deal with in detail, and it is a topic that deserves a chapter of its own (Chapter 5).

The sages believed that Adam and Eve lived in a vegetarian world. In Genesis and in Deuteronomy the earth's bounty is described in strictly vegetarian terms.

And God said, Behold, I have given you every herb yielding seed, which is upon the face of all the earth, and every tree, in the which is the fruit of a tree yielding seed; to you it shall be for food. . .[33]

For the Lord thy God bringeth thee into a good land, a land of brooks of water, of fountains and depths that spring out of valleys and hills; a land of wheat and barley, and vines, and fig trees, and pomegranates; a land of olive oil and honey; a land wherein thou shalt eat bread without scarceness, and thou shalt not lack any thing in it.[34]

The rabbis found it hard to imagine that the slaughtering of animals had taken place in the Garden of Eden. Nor could they imagine a Paradise without the pleasure of meat dishes! A legend of the Bible describes the angels bringing Adam, who had never killed an animal, "meat and wine, serving him like attendants."[35]

Only after the deluge were Noah and his children explicitly given permission to eat the flesh of animals. We are led to suppose that the display of human corruption and violence which led to the flood made it clear that man's appetite for flesh had become a fact of life, and it was better to permit and regulate the eating of flesh than to have men harbor a forbidden appetite that would again sow violence and corruption through human society.

As man was a vegetarian in his remotest origins, the prophets were sure that in times to come man would return once more to a vegetarian way of life.

> The wolf . . . shall dwell with the lamb, and the leopard shall lie down with the kid; and the calf and the young lion and fatling together; and a little child shall lead them. And the cow and the bear shall feed; their young ones shall lie down together; and the lion shall eat straw like the ox.[36]

The rabbis interpreted the permission to eat meat as a concession to human weakness. Both man's beginning and his destiny, Paradise and the time of the Messiah, are described in the Bible as vegetarian. Explicit rules of compassion toward animals, and dietary laws governing what kinds of animals man may eat and how he must slaughter and prepare them, were deemed necessary to govern human behavior through the corridor of time that would eventually lead to an era of peace among men, and peace between man and beast.

3

The Psychological Roots
of Human Compassion

Optimistically, perhaps, psychologists hope to learn something about human personality in general by examining one small aspect of behavior at a time. Sigmund Freud, for example, developed a theory of personality from his study of people who sought treatment for relief from emotional problems. What can we learn about human personality by studying how normal people in a variety of cultures relate to animals?

In commanding compassion to animals, for example, is the Bible endorsing and reinforcing a natural human tendency or does the commandment attempt to remake man from brute to angel?

Leaf through the reports of anthropologists who have visited preliterate societies untouched by the Biblical tradition and you will find an impressive number of cases in which food animals are treated with great affection. Simoons surveyed this literature and reports a number of such observations.[1] Take the Nambikwara Indians of Brazil, a people who "have many domesticated animals suitable for eating, and yet keep them simply as pets, sharing their food with them, and playing and talking to them. They do not even eat the eggs their hens lay.[2] Perhaps the care and affection we lavish on dogs would evoke a similar comment from a visitor from a dog-eating society. In many parts of the world dogs are not only considered "suitable for eating" but are regarded as a tonic or a delicacy. In China dog meat is called "fragrant meat," and the chow is believed to have been bred there as a meat animal.[3]

Back in 1898, Langkavel speculated that originally man domesticated the dog to obtain its flesh for food, and that at first this was the dog's major domestic role. The dog also served incidentally as a guard and, as pigs do today, as a scavenger.[4] Over the millennia, dogs were selectively bred as guards, hunters, workers, and companions. Dog-eating gradually became a matter of some ambivalence and finally came to be designated as "unnatural," taboo, a statutory crime.[5]

Simoons points to many groups where a bond of great affection develops between people and the animals they raise for work, hunting, or food. In China, for example, "a farmer who is forced by poverty to sell his [ox] took as great care in selecting a buyer as if he were finding a husband for his daughter, and was especially concerned that the animal should not fall into the hands of a butcher. The traditional opinion about butchers was that . . . the butcher's soul would be condemned eternally, and that his children, if he had any, would be poor and weak.[6]

The Sema Naga regard dog flesh as an "excellent tonic." Although a man will not eat his hunting dog, he will sell it for food when it is past usefulness.[7] "Besides ordinary village dogs, some Angami men own hunting dogs which they treat better and which they bury with honors. Though some dogs may be killed and eaten when they are too old to hunt, they are never eaten by the man who has trained or kept them."[8]

In Korea, dog meat is regarded as "a healthful food appropriate to the warm part of the year, and [some families] raise dogs for eating at that season." In some instances, families develop "too much affection for their household dogs to eat them at home. . . . [Instead] they will sell them for slaughter."[9]

Observers of the cattle peoples of East Africa report displays of "strong affection" and "loving reverence for their cattle." Cattle people have been observed to "pet and coax their cattle as if they were children and cry over their ailments . . . [to] sing and dance to their cattle in the evening."[10] "Occasionally the tie between man and beast has been so strong that the man has committed suicide on the death of his animal."[11]

DeVore and White observe that among Nomadic Tuareg of the Sahara, "the men are skilled hunters and they enjoy the sport of the hunt, but often they will purposely miss their target. . . . Weeks may go by without the taste of meat."[12] The authors conclude that the Tuaregs just "don't like to kill for food."[13]

Returning to the observations of Simoons, "among the Bari of the Sudan, when a man's favorite ox grows old and is ceremoniously killed, his friends eat the flesh, but the owner himself sits grief-stricken in his hut."[14] "In former days, childless Maori women of New Zealand sometimes carried and nursed young pigs as substitutes for their own offspring."[15]

In New Guinea, even a mature pig is fondled, petted, and treated with pride and affection. When finally it is killed, the woman who raised it "cries freely. The owner does not kill the pig, for as the Papuans say, sorrow would make his arm too weak to use his bow."[16]

Dudley Giehl describes several hunting societies which ceremonially express remorse or apology to the spirit of their prey. An eighteenth-century account of an Ottawa tribe of American Indians describes their plea to the spirit of a bear they killed: "Cherish us no grudge because we have killed you. You have sense; you see that our children are hungry." Giehl also notes that "certain North American Indian tribes wept for remorse for the buffalos they were about to kill." Similarly, an African tribe, when it kills an elephant in a hunt, offers an apology to the animal's spirit, "pretending its death was quite accidental."[17] Giehl also tells of the compassion that the Ainus of Sakhalin show toward the bear cubs they raise as meat animals. Before slaughtering one, a villager informs the bear "that he will be shot by the best archer so its death will be as quick and painless as possible. It is also told that it will now go to the 'god of the forest.' The archer who is assigned to kill the bear first asks the animal to forgive him and then weeps."[18]

But in the same anthropological surveys which report these tender ministrations of tribal peoples to domesticated animals, there are also described customs of shocking cruelty. Animals are reduced to lives of restricted activity so that they more readily grow fat—not only through castration, but by blinding them or by breaking their forelegs.[19] In a belief that the process tenderizes the flesh, animals are literally beaten to death or are singed over a fire while still alive.[20]

The task of animal slaughter can be guided by either man's capacity for compassion or by the impulse to hurt. Primitive cattle-keeping peoples do not necessarily become expert at quick and painless animal slaughter. Writes Erich Isaac: "I personally witnessed the strangling of a cow in Northern Rhodesia. The process took a long time. In some parts of Southern Rhodesia the animal is literally beaten to death with clubs."[21]

Cruelty to food animals is not confined to preliterate peoples. The Roman poet Horace "reported that a fowl drowned to death in wine had a particularly fine flavor."[22] In contemporary America, the production of milk-fed veal is described by Sussman as an exercise in unbelievable cruelty.

> Meat eaters fond of veal may think the pale, tender flesh they enjoy comes from a particular breed of calf. It does not. The so-called veal calf is an ordinary calf removed from its mother only three or four days after birth. . . .
> The calf is locked in a slatted stall. No bedding is provided for reasons that soon become clear. The stall is just large enough to let the calf stand or lie down. . . . It cannot even turn around in the stall. This treatment has a specific purpose. Pale, tender veal comes from a malnourished, anemic animal whose feed and movement are severely restricted. Allowed to move or exercise, allowed to feed on grass, grain or stall bedding, the calf would develop dark and toughened flesh. . . . To produce the heaviest animal in the shortest time . . . the producer will feed the calf an iron-deficient liquid diet based on a formula of dry milk and additives. The calf's water intake will be restricted to increase the appetite and to limit the iron content of the diet.
> But because the calf naturally craves iron, it may lick the iron fittings on its stall or attempt to lick its own urine. Veal producers combat this by tethering the calf's head and placing a bar behind its hind legs, further restricting its movement.
> . . . Unable to suck, ruminate, eat or drink properly . . . veal calves stand prisoners on the slotted floors of their dark stalls for three or four months. Because they are weak and susceptible to illness, they are dosed with antibiotics and drugs. They will leave their pens only when ready for slaughter.[23]

This description of methods of intensive veal production could be supplemented by recounting similarly cruel factory methods of chicken production, and by describing other refinements in meat production. The consumer becomes an unwitting partner in practices which would either horrify him or deaden his concern for the suffering of living creatures.

Today, civil laws forbid certain displays of cruelty to animals, and it was a British Jew, Lewis Gompertz, who introduced this kind of legislation to the Western world. In London, in the 1820s, Gompertz also founded the first Society for the Prevention of Cruelty to Animals.

In our own culture, baby animals readily evoke feelings of affection. Our impulse is to feed them, stroke them, protect them, play with them. Farmers become attached to their livestock, and many find it easier to sell off their livestock or hire an outsider to butcher and dress them than to slaughter and cut up the animals they have raised and grown attached to. People who visit Detroit want to tour an automobile plant. In Chicago, one of the world's largest bakeries conducts daily tours of its facilities. In Battle Creek, visitors want to see how breakfast foods are made. If you were passing through Omaha, would you enjoy visiting a slaughterhouse?

Simoons finds a widespread belief among primitive peoples "that slaughter is immoral and degrading, and that it contaminates the slaughterer."[24] Typically, "the butcher is placed in a position of danger and impurity but other people are thereby protected from contamination."[25]

Simoons describes the slaughterer's role in various societies. Among the Bemba of Northern Rhodesia (now Zambia), the butcher is a hereditary official who "undergoes purification ceremonies after the slaughter. The Gauche of the Canary Islands did not allow their professional butchers to enter the homes of other people . . . or to associate with anyone but those of their calling. In Japan, members of the butchers' caste . . . are regarded as unclean and kept from other people. The professional butchers in Tibet have been the most despised of all classes, regarded as professional sinners because they violate the Buddhist precept against taking life."[26]

In the Jewish culture, by contrast, the professional slaughterer, the *shochet*, is not an outcast, but occupies the elevated role of a clergyman-specialist. He is a person who combines moral rectitude, scholarly attainments, and the necessary manual dexterity for performing the act of animal slaughter according to strict Talmudic formula, with strokes so quick and deft that animal suffering is believed to be reduced to an absolute minimum. The role of the *shochet* is described more fully in Chapter 6.

Religious ceremony and animal slaughter are combined when the *shochet* recites a blessing beginning his daily work: "Blessed art thou, Lord our God, King of the universe, who has sanctified us with thy commandments and commanded us concerning *shechita*." After the animal has been slaughtered and its blood drained, the *shochet* examines the carcass to determine whether it is free from certain signs of sickness or mutilation which would render it unfit, *trefah*.[27]

Thus in one society the slaughterer of animals is ostracized as a professional sinner, and in another he is accorded the status of a religious functionary, chosen for both his manual dexterity and his religious piety, trained and licensed to implement the laws of *shechita*. Both customs stem from the feeling that animal slaughter is different from pruning vines or harvesting grain—that animal slaughter is potentially cruel and is not fit work for ordinary human beings. A scientific understanding of man would answer the question, How did man acquire this tendency to treat animals with compassion? Does it serve some biological function? The compassion that flowers in the Bible, where is it rooted in human nature?

It seems unlikely that nature would so lavishly endow living creatures with drives that lead to procreation and neglect to implant in them instincts which would insure the necessary care and protection of their young. For the impulse to procreate contributes nothing to the survival of the species unless the young survive their stage of infantile helplessness.

Animals of all kinds seem to be programmed by nature to protect and care for their young. The protective and nurturing behavior of animal parents is marvelous to behold. Compared with other living creatures, man has a much longer period of infantile helplessness. At first glance, it may seem like a biological defect that the human infant remains utterly helpless at an age when young chimpanzees are already scampering about and looking after their needs. Undoubtedly, however, the slow rate of human growth is more of a strength than a weakness, allowing the human nervous system to develop as an organ of learning as well as a repository of instinct.

If there is a biological value to the human infant's slow rate of development, then we must suppose that this characteristic could not have developed unless there also developed strong tendencies for able-bodied humans to respond to helplessness with compassion, to offer an abundance of protective, loving care.[28]

This is a law of evolution—that related changes must occur in synchrony. Just as the capacity for eye-hand coordination developed through synchronized changes in the eye and in the hand, human infancy could be extended only as more mature humans displayed an ever-greater tendency toward compassion toward the helpless. These are the biological roots of which the Biblical rules of compassion—to one's neighbor, to the stranger, to the poor, to animals—are the flowers.

One of the far-reaching implications of the human infant's prolonged period of infantile helplessness is that man is "genetically programmed," as it is fashionable to say, to express an extraordinary degree of compassion.

Do we profane the impulse of compassion by tracing it to a by-product of infantile helplessness? No more than we disparage the love of a husband for his wife by bringing up the sexual side of marriage. No more than we belittle the beauty of a pearl by describing it as an oyster's defense against an irritant. The scientific question may be, Where did it come from? But the moral question is, What shall we do with it?

Sigmund Freud, however far-reaching his insights on the human psyche, did not share the view that compassion is intrinsic to human nature. Freud believed that all human tendencies could be traced to two basic drives—lust and aggression, and that justice and mercy were rules imposed by society in its attempt to civilize man. The theme of Freud's *Civilization and Its Discontents* is that man has become a captive of civilization, chafing with discontent because his impulses of lust and aggression oppose the interests of society, and must therefore be forever thwarted. Freud believed that the commandment to love your neighbor was an attempt to counteract man's basic drive toward aggression. He believed that man's instinct was stronger than social rules, and that this laudable effort to remake man was doomed to failure.[29]

From our point of view, the commandment to love your neighbor is an extension of the impulse of compassion for the helpless—an impulse as instinctive as lust or aggression. Displacement of affect follows the laws of psychoanalysis, as stimulus-generalization follows the laws of experimental psychology. And compassion for animals represents another outpouring of an inborn human tendency.

Why, then, is compassion for animals—and humans!—not more widely practiced? Why do men kill for food, hunt for sport, and visit unnecessary cruelty on their fellow human beings? Because as real as the impulse for compassion may be, antagonistic impulses are also real. The human psyche contains a potential for both loving-kindness and cruelty, for both impulses to help and impulses to hurt. It is erroneous to say that one side is biologically rooted and the other side is a social artifact. Both sides spring from the depths of human nature.

It is likewise erroneous to suppose that some peoples or some social groups are genetically predisposed toward either compassion or cruelty. A thousand years ago the Vikings were the scourge and terror of Europe and England (and they held drinking bouts using mugs made from the skulls of their enemies). Today, their genetic descendants, the Scandinavians, are a model of a peace-loving people.

Before Israel became a state, it was common wisdom that the Zionist idea would fail because the Jew would not defend his soil, that centuries of ghetto life had undone any potential for physical combat the Jew had ever had. Subsequent events showed that common wisdom does not predict how human events will unfold. Historical realities help determine which of a person's vast potentials are actualized at any moment in history.

National perils and ambitions rise and fall. Individual feelings of threat rise and fall, and with these vicissitudes man's aggressive potential sometimes becomes actualized into dominant attitudes, habits, and goals. If eternal human strivings can be seen above the changing, shifting human scene, perhaps Paul Bohannon offers a glimpse of them when he writes, in his *Social Anthropology*, that the basic tenet of all major religions of the world is that "unselfishness is the primary virtue and that selfishness lies at the root of the world's ills.[30]

Acts of selfishness must be defended, disguised, rationalized, restructured, to make them acceptable even to oneself. In *Passions and Constraints*, van den Haag points out that before a people can treat an enemy with cruelty, it is common to deny that the enemy is even human—the enemy must first be redefined as subhuman, bestial, scum.[31] Acts of compassion, on the other hand, do not need to be explained or disguised—"I did it because I wanted to help." Hypocrisy is the tribute that vice pays to virtue.

In *The Merchant of Venice*, a female lawyer appeals to a judge's compassion with the words:

The quality of mercy is not strain'd,
It droppeth as the gentle rain from heaven
Upon the place beneath. It is twice bless'd:
It blesseth him that gives and him that takes.

Was Portia displaying a skillful use of rhetoric to save her client's life, or was she correct in saying that compassion is, after all, a natural and normal human tendency? What Shakespeare intuited long ago, we now have four hundred more years of experience to confirm.

4

The Craving for Flesh

Only after the deluge does God explicitly give Noah and his sons permission to eat the flesh of animals, fowl, and fish.

> The fear of you and the dread of you shall be upon every beast of the earth, and upon every fowl of the air . . . and upon all the fishes of the sea; into your hands are they delivered. Every moving thing that liveth shall be for food for you; as the green herb have I given you all. Only . . . blood . . . shall ye not eat.[1]

How can one reconcile the pro-vegetarian statements contained in the first chapters of Genesis, and the recurrent theme of compassion for animals expressed throughout the Bible, with this explicit permission to eat animal flesh? The sages pondered over this and took a clue from the statement that between the times of Adam and Noah, the earth became "corrupt . . . and filled with violence."[2] Did this display of corruption include cannibalism? The Bible does not say. Did it include the tearing of limbs from living beasts? The drinking of blood? Probably, because both these practices are explicitly forbidden in the Bible.

In his essay "A Vision of Peace and Vegetarianism," Rabbi Abraham Isaac Kook carefully examines the question of how the Laws of Moses could at the same time put such emphasis on compassion toward animals and permit the slaughter of animals for food. Rabbi Kook argues that the corruption and violence which led up to the flood made it clear that

17

because man had an insatiable desire to eat flesh, he could not yet be held to a moral standard which excluded the eating of flesh. Noah and his sons were given permission to eat the flesh of certain animals "after all the desires of thy soul."[3] Let us remember that the Laws of Noah were intended for *all* mankind, and that the Laws of Moses were intended for *all* the children of Israel. Laws which could be successfully adopted by a cult or a sect might be altogether unworkable for an entire people, and this is as true today as it was in the time of Noah.

In his essay "The Dietary Prohibitions of the Hebrews," Soler sees in the Bible two occasions on which an attempt was made to try the Hebrew people out on a vegetarian regime.[4] During the period of the flight from Egypt, when the Hebrews lived exclusively on manna, they had large flocks which they did not touch. Manna is described as a vegetable food—"like coriander seed."[5] "Twice, however, the men rebelled against Moses because they wanted to eat meat."[6] Lamented the meat-hungry Hebrews, "Would that we had died by the hand of the Lord in the land of Egypt, when we sat by the flesh-pots." God ended the "experiment in vegetarianism" by manifesting the miracle of the quails.

A second "experiment in vegetarianism" is suggested in the Book of Numbers, when again the Hebrews lament, "O that we had meat to eat." God repeats the miracle of the quails, this time with great wrath—"You shall not eat one day, or two days, or five days, or ten days, or twenty days, but a whole month, until it comes out of your nostrils and becomes loathsome to you."[7] Solar notes that then "a great number of Hebrews . . . fall upon the quails and gorge themselves [and] die on the spot. Here, as in the myth of the Flood, meat is given a negative connotation. It is a concession God makes to man's imperfection."[8]

Man's moral imperfection is still a fact in today's world, says Rabbi Kook, as it was also true in the time of Job, who described his contemporary as "abominal and filthy . . . one who drinketh iniquity like water."[9] Modern man is no different, says Rabbi Kook. "Man is still ruled by tyranny and falsehood, nationalistic hatreds and jealousies, racial hatreds, and family feuds, over which rivers of blood continue to be spilled."[10]

Man was not ready to follow a vegetarian ethic in the time of Noah or in the time of Job, says Rabbi Kook, and is still not ready in the contemporary world. In his present moral condition, man could not tolerate a ban against killing animals. Perhaps, Rabbi Kook warns, it would be dangerous to make animal flesh and human flesh equally forbidden! The irrational craving for flesh might even lead to the slaughtering of humans for food.[11]

Rabbi Kook points out that nowhere in the Bible is cannibalism forbidden. It is not necessary, he observes, to explicitly prohibit what is already "loathsome to man's deepest nature." The time will come, says Rabbi Kook, when man will live on a moral plane which will make the eating of animal flesh likewise repugnant.

Rabbi Kook expresses his conviction that the custom of eating animal flesh was never intended for all time. "For how can it be that a moral position [expressed in the words of Genesis 1:29] so noble and enlightened . . . should pass away after it once has been brought into existence?"[12]

Rabbi Kook regards cannibalism as "loathsome to man's deepest nature," yet several times in his "Vision" essay he expresses the fear that a ban on the eating of animal flesh might result in cannibalism. This speculation is supported by many signs—the prominence of cannibalism themes in the mythology of Greece[13] and other peoples, in the fairy tales we read our children,[14] and in observed practices on every continent of the world.

The blood-accusation against Mendel Beilis in Kiev in 1911 and against his many predecessors was altogether plausible to the European mind in the light of man's long record of consuming human flesh and blood. Cannibalism seems to have been a routine practice in the prehistoric world,[15] was known in ancient China,[16] and was witnessed among the Aztecs[17] and in various other places in the world.

In times of famine, reports of cannibalism are not uncommon. Such incidents are a footnote to ancient and modern times of crisis.[18]

In 1846 George Donner left Utah with a party of over 100 people, to find a shortcut to California. They encountered unbelievable hardships in waterless miles of salt desert and mountain blizzards. Half of the party lived to see California, but the price they paid included murder, madness, and cannibalism. Without eating human flesh, "none of the Donner party would have survived."[19]

In his memoirs, Nikita Khrushchev recalls a description of cannibalism observed during the Ukrainian famine of 1947.

The woman had a corpse of her own child on the table and was cutting it up. She was chattering away as she worked. "We've already eaten Marechka [little Maria]. Now we'll salt down Vanechka [little Ivan]. This will keep us for some time." Can you imagine? This woman had gone crazy with hunger and butchered her own children![20]

The Andes crash of 1972 represents a recent and well-documented case of cannibalism. Disaster struck a plane flying from Montevideo to Santiago, carrying fifteen young rugby players and twenty-five of their friends and relations, for a series of games. When the plane crashed among the peaks of the Andes, seven died from the crash or from an avalanche that struck the fuselage. Thirty-two "survived seventy days in the bitter heights of the Andes by eating the flesh of their dead companions." One survivor of the crash died of starvation because he could not bring himself to eat human flesh. Tannahill reports: "The crash victims passed from revulsion to acceptance, and then to enjoyment of their new diet. . . . They even began to develop gourmet tastes, favoring the brains and lungs . . . relishing the piquant flavor of flesh that had begun to decay."[21]

Some of the incidents recounted above took place after the time of Rabbi Kook. How much did he know of the history of cannibalism, or did he merely intuit that eating human flesh was well within the repertory of human behavior, and that the prospect of famine—and cannibalism—would have increased if the ancient Hebrews, a pastoral people, had somehow been forced to give up cattle-raising?

The lamentation of the meat-hungry Hebrews during their flight from Egypt, pining for the flesh-pots of Egypt ("Would that we were given flesh to eat!"), has a parallel in the behavior of some tribes that suffer from an occasional scarcity or absence of meat. The Bemba of Northern Rhodesia have a special word, *ubukashya*, for the craving of meat. When the Lele of the Congo have no meat or fish to eat, they lose interest in eating and may instead "choose to drink palm wine and go to sleep without eating."[22] Among the Ojibway, a meat famine brings with it the risk of succumbing to a psychotic craving for human flesh. This madness is believed to be induced by the Windigo, a cannibal giant who resides in the woods.[23]

It is quite possible that vulnerability to these cravings and crazes for meat-eating, like vulnerability to the protein-deficiency disease *kwashiorkor*, is peculiar to peoples who are not only deprived of meat but also have no access to alternative full-protein sources—eggs, cheese, or grain-legume combinations. Perhaps it was famine experiences like those described above, plus the absence of adequate protein-food alternatives, that accounts for the ancient Hebrews' strong association of meat-eating with well-being. Still the Bible contains the recollection of a primordial vegetarianism and the dream of a return to this vegetarianism in the time of the Messiah, when "the lion shall eat straw like the ox."[24]

5

Slaughter as a Mode of Worship

In the 1969 edition of the *Encyclopaedia Britannica*, Leviticus is called the book of the Hebrew Bible "seldomest read and least admired. . . . It contains dull, repetitious listings and uninteresting details about a sacrificial system no longer observed by either Christians or Jews." The *New Jewish Encyclopedia*[1] likewise gives only eighteen lines to its entry on Leviticus—compared with fifty-five lines for its entry on Isaiah and twenty-four lines for its entry on the Book of Psalms.

With the destruction of the Temple in 70 c.e., the sacrificial system presumably came to an end, and Jewish religious life moved from Temple altars and priests and sacrifices to synagogues and rabbis, study and prayer. Does Leviticus represent an orientation which the Jewish religion has indeed outgrown and has no more interest in? Certain facts suggest that, on the contrary, Leviticus has had a sizable influence on post-Biblical Jewish thought and daily practice. Why? What is the central moral problem of Leviticus, and how does this problem touch our lives today?

The hidden influence of Leviticus is suggested by a statement by Rabbi Joseph Milgrom that nearly half (247) of the 613 commandments are based upon Leviticus, and that the same proportion of the Talmud deals with problems raised in Leviticus. To further demonstrate "the impact of Leviticus on Judaism," Rabbi Milgrom points out that "traditionally the first book taught to school children" was *Va'yikra*, or Leviticus.

A major content of Leviticus is animal slaughter as a vehicle of worship. Doesn't this seem like an unlikely mode of worship to a God who commands compassion to all his creatures? To come to grips with this monumental paradox, it is necessary to keep in mind two facts about the world of ancient Israel:

1. The tribes of Israel were a pastoral people and therefore a flesh-eating people.
2. They inhabited a world in which blood sacrifices, both animal and human, were widely practiced.

Human sacrifice, writes Rabbi Hertz, was a religious practice "rife among the Semitic peoples, as well as their Egyptian and Aryan neighbours."[2] In the ancient world, the sacrifice of animals was perhaps as well-established a mode of religious worship as the singing of hymns or the reciting of prayers is today. Rabbi Hertz argues that the sacrificial cult was so essential to ancient religious practice that unless the laws of Moses included this "universal expression of religious homage," the mission of Moses "would assuredly have failed, and his work would have disappeared."[3]

One indication that animal sacrifice was a familiar practice in the ancient world is that nowhere in Leviticus, or anywhere else in the Bible, is the ritual of animal sacrifice formally explained. It is dealt with as a self-evident and familiar practice. Like prayer, animal sacrifice is accepted as a "universally current expression of religious homage."[4]

What functions did human and animal sacrifice serve in the pagan religions? Let us conjecture that human sacrifice symbolized the awesome power of the group over the individual and, at the same time, the willingness of the tribe to surrender what was most precious to it, in order to propitiate its gods. Let us suppose that animal sacrifice was intended to actually nourish the gods, to entreat them, and to win their lasting favor.

Let us accept Rabbi Hertz's conjecture that the sacrificial cult was too prominent a feature of religious worship to be cast aside. Instead, the shapers of the Hebrew religion ventured to radically restructure the sacrificial cult, replacing pagan values with Judaic values—monotheism, holiness, compassion.[5] Accordingly, the sacrificial cult of the Hebrews was governed by the following six rules:

1. Human sacrifice was banned completely. The binding of Isaac may be read as a statement that God does not want children to be

sacrificed. The ram caught in the thicket suggested to Abraham that he could substitute an animal as a blood offering to God.

Significantly, God does not command Abraham to sacrifice the ram. In the Bible story, Abraham sees the ram caught in the thicket, and concludes that it can serve as a substitute for his son.

Leviticus contains this specific prohibition against child sacrifice—" Whosoever he be of the children of Israel, or of the strangers that sojourn in Israel, that giveth his seed [children] unto Molech; he shall surely be put to death."[6]

2. Blood rituals were limited to the offering of animals deemed fit for consumption. Fit—*kashar* (from which word the terms *kashrut* and *kosher* are derived)—for the diet of a holy people are only those animals which are thorough herbivores, grazing animals, animals that "chew the cud."

Hoofed feet were given as signs of a grazing animal, as claws betoken an animal that seizes its prey. Carnivores were deemed unfit or unclean, comments Soler, because such an animal "has itself consumed meat and killed other animals in order to do so. . . . If man were to eat them, he would be doubly unclean."[7] Thus, the restriction of meat-eating to the flesh of grazing animals only, may be seen as a step toward vegetarianism.

3. Only the Temple priests could conduct animal sacrifices, and the themes of these rituals would be atonement and thanksgiving — atonement for various transgressions of the Law, and atonement for the very act of animal slaughter!

4. As in pagan rituals of animal slaughter, the carcasses would eventually be eaten by the worshippers, but Hebrew law set limits to feasting upon animal flesh—there could be no drinking of blood (for blood was held to symbolize the essence of life, and was to be returned to the Giver of life) and no gorging upon fat.

5. The sacrifice of animals would be supplemented by the offering of doves and pigeons, offerings which were within reach of the poor.

(Otherwise Temple offerings were to a large extent what Thorstein Veblen would call "conspicuous consumption.")

Interestingly, it is specified in Leviticus that the priest himself should carry out every bird offering. Kalish conjectures that this rule was intended "to enhance the importance of the poor man's offering."[8]

6. Animal sacrifices would be supplemented by "vegetarian offerings" —first fruits, and cakes baked of fine flour.

The Hebrew word for an offering, or a sacrifice, is *korban*, which stems from the Hebrew word *karav* and means "to come close." *Korban* may thus be translated as "that which is brought near." It is an ambiguous or multivocal word. It could mean, in a literal sense, "that which is brought near to God by presentation upon the Temple altar," or it could mean, "that which brings the giver closer to the presence of God."

Thus, Leviticus radically transforms the pagan ritual of animal sacrifice, and uses this ritual to confront man with the towering contradiction between his appetite for animal flesh and God's designation of life as something sacred. Animal sacrifice, once an occasion for indulging in magical, sadistic, and gluttonous impulses, is transformed into a rite of atonement performed by Temple priests.

Animal sacrifice may represent the most provocative *content* of the Book of Leviticus, but the central problem of the book is how to transform the Israelites into a holy people.[9] Five times, the command is repeated: "Ye shall be holy, for I am holy." The word *kodesh*, meaning "holiness" or "holy," appears in Leviticus about 150 times.

Holiness is defined in part by various kinds of renunciation—renunciation of certain sexual practices (incest, bestiality, homosexuality) and renouncing of the ungoverned indulgence in animal flesh. A compromise is made between the vegetarian ideal—symbolized in man's mythical origin and destiny—and the reality of man's appetite for animal flesh, by designating as clean only grazing animals (vegetarian animals!). Prohibited are animals which have died of themselves, or were killed by another beast. Before animal flesh can be eaten, the carcass must be drained of blood, for blood is the essence of life and must therefore be returned to the Giver of life. Along with the blood, the choicest bits of the carcass, the internal fat,[10] must also be offered to God rather than be eaten.

Rabbi Milgrom interprets the blood prohibition as a rule which enables man to "indulge his lust for meat and not be brutalized in the process." Rabbi Milgrom adds, "Many prophets sharply criticized the sacrificial system when it failed to lead to a more ethical life, but their lonely isolation in this respect and the positive evidence of the folk literature make it amply clear that the people themselves were convinced that it met their spiritual needs."[11]

The quest for holiness does not end by substituting animal sacrifice for infant sacrifice, by transforming animal slaughter into a sacred rite of thanksgiving or atonement, or even by reconciling man's appetite for animal flesh with his worship of a God who has mercy on all his creatures. The quest for holiness must include rules of compassion toward all human beings, toward all the poor and unsettled, toward Hebrew and stranger alike.

The tone of Leviticus is not merely to evoke sympathy for the suffering of the poor, but to command specific practices from which the poor would benefit: for example, the commandments not to harvest the corners of one's field, not to gather fallen fruits, not to glean one's vineyard or grain field, not to delay in giving a hired servant his pay, not to take sexual advantage of a betrothed maiden, and not to wrong the stranger—"Thou shalt love him as thyself; for ye were strangers in the land of Egypt,"[12] This sentiment, to "love the stranger as thyself," is translated into a specific commandment: "Ye shall have one manner of law, as well for the stranger, as for the home-born."[13]

In the same part of Leviticus, known as the holiness section, appear the three Hebrew words which are translated as "Thou shalt love thy neighbor as thyself": וְאָהַבְתָּ לְרֵעֲךָ כָּמוֹךְ. The modern reader of Leviticus, who is at turns bored and offended by the endless details of carrying out animal sacrifices, experiences astonishment and awe to discover the "golden rule" in tandem with harsh and alien rules of animal sacrifice.[14]

A Catholic scholar, Rev. Robert North, S.J., in his *Encyclopaedia Britannica* article on Leviticus, acknowledges that this law is indeed "considered to be a Christian innovation and the most distinctive of Jesus' teachings—Love your neighbor as yourself."[15] "Love thy neighbor" has a special meaning for vegetarians, who look upon their dietary practice as an expression of concern for the poorer peoples of the world, and see in vegetarianism a more equitable sharing of the world's food resources. For Jewish vegetarians it is important to know the Jewish roots of "the most distinctive of Jesus' teachings."

In addition to asking for mercy for the poor and displaced, Leviticus commands "reverence for parents . . . honorable dealing. no tale-bearing or malice . . . just measures and balances—together with abhorrence of everything unclean, irrational or heathen. Holiness is thus attained not by flight from the world, nor by monk-like renunciation of human relationships of family or station, but by the spirit in which we fulfil the obligations of life in its simplest and commonest details: in this way—by doing justly, loving mercy, and walking humbly with our God—is everyday life transfigured."[16] Rabbi Hertz is saying that while the Temple offering section of Leviticus deals with a ritual which stands outside of everyday experience, the holiness section of Leviticus advocates a hallowing of the everyday—an important theme in Jewish vegetarianism.

If the Temple offering section of Leviticus and the holiness section represent an attempt to tie together a Dionysian and an Apollonian tradition,[17] this attempt did not last for long. The moral offensiveness with which Temple offerings came to be regarded is expressed in the words of the prophets and psalmists.

> Your countless sacrifices, what are they to me?
> says the Lord.
> I am sated with whole-offerings of rams
> and the fat of buffaloes;
> I have no desire for the blood of bulls,
> of sheep and of he-goats.

> The offer of your gifts is useless,
> the reek of sacrifice is abhorrent to me.[18]

> Loyalty is my desire, not sacrifice,
> not whole-offerings but the knowledge of God.[19]

> God, the Lord God, has spoken
> and summoned the world from the rising to the setting sun . . . .

Shall I not find fault with your sacrifices
though your offerings are before me always?
I need take no young bull from your house,
   no he-goat from your folds;
for all the beasts of the forest are mine
   and the cattle in thousands on my hills.
If I were hungry, I would not tell you,
   for the world and all that is in it are mine.
Shall I eat the flesh of your bulls
   or drink the blood of he-goats?[20]

Jeremiah scolds those who "steal, murder, and commit adultery, and swear falsely, and burn incense unto Baal" and then come to the Temple and make "burnt-offerings . . . and eat flesh." God could only comment, says Jeremiah, that "the children of Judah have done evil in my sight . . . they have set abominations in the house which is called by my name, to pollute it."[21]

Greeks and Christians likewise looked down upon the excesses of the sacrificial system of the Hebrews.[22] With the destruction of the Temple in 70 c.e., the sacrificial system came to an end. Now religious worship was expressed in synagogue prayer, in study, and in acts of righteousness. The holiness section expressed the dominant spirit of the Hebrew religion:

Acts of justice are more meritorious than all the sacrifices.
Unless the mind is purified, the sacrifice is useless; it may
be thrown to the dogs.[23]

He who prays is considered as pious as if he had built an
altar and offered sacrifices upon it.[24]

One might suppose that the animal-sacrifice section of Leviticus became a historical curiosity. But so long as animals were slaughtered for food, there would remain the impulse to atone for this act, in those who worship a God for whom all life is sacred. This is the spiritual need that the sacrificial system once met. It is the thesis of the next chapter that the dietary laws of the diaspora emerged as a *replacement* for the sacrificial system, and that the Temple priest was replaced by the diaspora *shochet*.

6

The Dietary Laws as Atonements for Flesh-Eating

How can a God who has mercy on all that lives permit the slaughter of animals for food?[1] In the days of the Temple, this towering incongruity was resolved by making a religious ritual out of the embarrassing task of animal slaughter, and by assigning the task to Temple priests. Animals were slaughtered to celebrate the glory of God, and only secondarily to satisfy the appetites of the worshippers. The ceremony contained its own acts of atonement. Choice portions of the carcass, and in some cases entire carcasses, were sacrificed to God upon a flaming altar. Blood, believed to contain the essence of life, was ceremonially separated from the flesh. The blood was returned to the Giver of life. With wine, bread, and music, the lifeless flesh was transformed into a banquet of thanksgiving.

With the fall of Jerusalem in 70 C.E. came the destruction of the Temple, the disappearance of the priestly slaughterers, and an end to the recurring drama which transformed animal slaughter into a holy celebration. With the loss of a national life, loss of kin, loss of homes, loss of worldly goods, loss of livelihood, and loss of the Temple which was a monument to their faith, the survivors must have been engulfed by an overwhelming sense of mourning, and must have been assailed by insecurities and doubts concerning many things that in normal times had been taken for granted.

Above all, an enormous sense of mourning must have hung over the surviving remnant. A mourner loses his appetite and his interest in the joys of living. For the expression of these feelings, a number of mourners must have been attracted to the ascetic cults of ancient Israel, which had already existed for quite some time before the destruction. The Qumran group associated with the Dead Sea Scrolls appears to have already disappeared, but there were others—Nazirites, Rechabites, Essenes, Therapeutae, and Zadokites. With the destruction of the Temple, the ascetic cults must have expressed as never before a predominant mood of the people.

A central feature of some of these ascetic groups was abstinence from the eating of meat. Celibacy, fasting, and other forms of privation also marked the ascetic regimen, but vegetarianism was a prominent symbol of the ascetic life, and was now fittingly associated with mourning for the destruction of the Temple.

Feasting on meat was once the sequel to a Temple ceremony, the ascetics reasoned. Now that the Temple is in ruins, and its priestly slaughterers are dispersed, how can we eat meat? The rabbis took this argument very seriously. The very survival of the Jews as a people must have seemed threatened by the ascendance of sects which withdrew into monkish, celibate lives and advocated abstinence from life-supporting dietary practices. The Talmud documents the rabbis' concern over the ascetic arguments, and over the growing numbers of adherents to the ascetic sects.

Following the destruction of the Temple, the number of recluses who would not eat meat or drink wine increased in Israel.[2]

The ascetics argued: "When the Temple was standing, our joy was in eating meat, as it is writen, "Thou shalt kill of thy peace offerings and eat them there and rejoice before the Lord thy God.' Now, when the Temple is destroyed, we [can] rejoice only in the drinking of wine."[3]

The Talmud documents how the rabbis debated back and forth over whether to prohibit the eating of meat and the drinking of wine as a perpetual sign of mourning for the destruction of the Temple. Finally, the rabbis decided to reject the ascetic argument. Judaism, after all, was a religion of life, and "the rabbis [considered] asceticism and privation as a sin against the will of God, [and believed] that people should enjoy the gift of life."[4]

Rabbi Ishmael ben Elisha is quoted as saying: "Since the destruction of the Temple, we should deny ourselves meat and wine. But we should not impose an ordinance unless the community can abide by it."[5] Rabbi Joshua agreed: "It is impossible to refrain from mourning altogether in view of the ruin visited upon us. But it is also impractical to impose mourning usages that are too stringent. Regulations that are too onerous for the community to bear should not be imposed."⁶

However undocumented, it is altogether likely that a factor which strongly contributed to the Talmudic rabbis' opposition to vegetarianism was their first-hand observation of the long-term effects of a meatless diet on its ascetic practitioners. The "maudlin vegetarianism"⁷ of that time probably produced visible signs of undernourishment, malnourishment, stunted growth, and deficiency diseases. To observers who wanted to see the Jewish people survive and raise a healthy new generation, this sight of sickly vegetarian ascetics must have delivered a frightening warning that the Jewish people could literally die away unless they were once more given a way to hallow the eating of meat.

As a compromise, the rabbis designated a specifically vegetarian period of nine days preceding the ninth day of the month of Ab—Tisha B'av—the anniversary of the destruction, still known among traditional Jews as "the meatless days." There has also been a tradition among observant Jews of advocating perpetual vegetarianism for Jews who live in the city of Jerusalem.

To make a place for animal slaughter in the religious life of the Jews, and make meat-eating fitting for a holy people, the rabbis assigned the role of the community *shochet* as a replacement for the Temple priest-slaughterer, and in the Talmud set forth in great detail the subtle and complex rules of animal slaughter which had been practiced by the Temple priests. And by elaborating a complex system of dietary laws, the rabbis gave every Jew a role in sanctifying the everyday acts of food preparation and eating.

When we read or think about the fact that with the fall of Jerusalem, the religious practices of the Jews shifted from Temple ritual to synagogue study and prayer, our attention usually focuses upon a break, a shift of direction, a *discontinuity* in the religious life of the Jews. Now, however, we can see the bridge, the link, the *continuity* between Temple ritual and synagogue study! For in the synagogues, the rabbis pondered the question —How can the Jews remain a holy people *without* their Temple rituals, and especially without their ritual of atonement for the eating of meat? Their answer was to meticulously document the role of the *shochet* and a system of dietary laws.

There were no *shochtim* in the days of the Bible. Any adult Jew of normal intelligence was permitted to slaughter an animal if he observed the prevailing rules of *kashrut*.[8] What were these practices? The Talmudic rabbis maintained that the *shechita* laws, which they were putting into writing for the first time, had been given to Moses by God, and that Moses taught the details of kosher animal slaughter "to his people by word of mouth, and they in turn transmitted them from generation to generation."[9]

It is believed that the *shechita* rules set forth in the Talmud document the oral tradition that had been followed by the Temple priests. These rules are so subtle and complex that their faithful administration requires the services of a carefully selected and trained clergyman-specialist. In Biblical times, could any adult Jew of normal intelligence carry out the complex rules of *shechita*?

Rabbi Seymour E. Freedman describes the *shochet* as a person of special physical, mental, and moral gifts, one who is carefully selected and trained to protect the health of the community.

> The person who becomes a *shochet* cannot be someone from the dregs of society who slaughters simply because he can wield a poleaxe, or thrust a sword coldbloodedly into the heart of a steer, or shoot it in the head. He cannot be someone who *must* do the work of a slaughterer because he can't find any other means of employment. A *shochet* is a scholar whose training is designed to make him sensitive and humble. He is a religious person whose commitment is to a life of sanctity. His is a profession, a high calling. He performs a holy task and offers a prayer before he begins his work, to alert himself to the presence of the divine spirit whose messenger he now is. . . .
>
> . . . His training is most exacting, so that when he is finally presented the *t'udah* (his diploma), he will represent in the market place and the community at large the highest standards of the Jewish ethic of compassion and humaneness. This is the spiritual image of the man who stands ready to slaughter an animal with God as his judge.
>
> . . . Like other Jewish clergy—rabbis and cantors—the *shochet* studies the *Shulchan Aruch* (Jewish Code of Law) in depth. From the specialized Talmudic tractate of Hulin, he learns the anatomy of the cow and the chicken. He can distinguish between the healthy and the sick.[10]

The *shochet* learns how to cut an animal's jugular vein with a gentle, rapid, and unhesitating to-and-fro motion, avoiding these five errors.

1. Delay—*shebiah*. The *shochet* applies his knife to the correct spot for severing the jugular vein, without halting. Prolonging the act of slaughtering whether intentionally or unintentionally would render the meat unkosher.[11]
2. Excessive pressure—*derash*. The cut may cleanly sever the gullet and windpipe as well as the jugular vein, but the knife should not scrape against the vertebrae. Again the theme of compassion shows through, to render the animal unconscious with a minimum of bodily insult and pain.
3. Obstruction of view—*baladah*. The *shochet* must at all times see what he is doing, unobstructed by darkness or by his own garments.
4. Deviation—*hagrama*. The *shochet* studies and follows the Talmud's careful descriptions of the glandular and cartilaginous protuberances on the animal's throat, which enables him to find the exact location at which to slide his blade. An incision above or below the designated line is considered mutilation and the slaughtering is non-kosher.
5. Tearing—*ikkur*. If examination of the carcass shows that the gullet and windpipe are not only severed but torn away from their supporting tissue, the animal becomes unfit for food.[12] To avoid painful tearing, the *shochet* keeps his knife sharp and smooth, perfectly free from any notch. Periodically the community rabbi inspects the *shochet's* knife to make sure it is perfectly smooth.

The rules of *shechita* make it "a significantly religious act," argues Rabbi Jeremiah Berman, an act that calls for a "sensitive and reverential" religious specialist.

In Judaism the act of animal slaying is not viewed as a step in the business of meat preparation. It is a deed charged with religious import. It is felt that the flame of animal life partakes of the sacred, and may be extinguished only by the sanction of religion, and only at the hands of one of its sensitive and reverential servants. The performance of *shechita* is, as every Jew who follows the tradition senses, a significantly religious act.[13]

The same writer correctly observes, "No more eloquent proof of the high place the *shochet* held—in the estimation of the Jew—can be furnished than to say that in many communities the *shochet* was also the cantor, teacher, or rabbi."[14]

A Hasidic tale dramatizes the tension contained in a way of life that both commands compassion for animals and designates a ritual of animal slaughter.

> A revered and saintly figure, the old *shochet* died, and the village elders were looking for a replacement. One of the elders interviewed a candidate and watched him perform the *shechita* ritual. Asked another elder—"Were you satisfied with the demonstration? Did he do it well? The observer gave a long sigh. "What's the matter?" asked the other. "Did he not do everything correctly? Was there something wrong with how he recited the prayer? . . . sharpened the knife? . . . moisten-ed the blade?"
>
> "Our old *shochet*," answered the other, "moistened the blade with his tears."

Whenever it is argued that the *shochet* must be a person of unusual gifts, temperament, and training, an assertion that is easily supported by facts, that argument inadvertently supports this author's thesis that in Biblical times Jews could *not* have employed all the rituals of *shechita*, for at that time animal slaughter could be performed by any normal adult. Hence we see the *shochet* as a priestlike role established by the Talmudic rabbis to sanction the eating of animal flesh by a people who worshipped a God of compassion, a people who once had a Temple priesthood to symbolize the moral correctness of animal slaughter.

To further undo the moral wrong that is committed by taking an animal's life for food purposes, the Talmudic rabbis evolved and documented a complex system of rules of *kashrut*, or dietary laws, govern-ing the preparation and eating of meat.

True, it may be argued that the dietary laws *originate* in the Biblical commands against unclean foods and against seething a calf in its mother's milk. But as Erich Isaac has pointed out, the Bible is equally explicit about many other everyday practices—not rounding the corners of one's beard, wearing fringed garments, renouncing sexual aberrations, renouncing false weights and measures. Many of the Biblical commands are untouched by rabbinical elaboration, and others are actually played down. (For example, it is permissible to wear fringes underneath the outer garments.) The extraordinary elaboration of the food prohibitions, therefore, calls for an interpretation, and our interpretation is that the dietary laws, like *shechita*, were evolved to replace the sacrificial system of atonements for killing God's creatures.

For example, the laws of *kashrut* require that to free the meat from blood, it must be salted and soaked in water, not once but several times—a treatment which reduces the quality of the meat significantly by gourmet standards. Rabbi Freedman describes this regimen.

> *First*, the meat is soaked in cold water for a half-hour in order to soften the meat so that the blood will come out easily and, in addition to remove any surface blood on the meat. *Second*, the meat is carefully salted on all its sides and in its crevices. The salt that is used must be coarser than ordinary table salt so that it will not deteriorate before the task of removing the blood has been completed. *Third*, the salt that has become saturated with the withdrawn blood is washed off by soaking the meat momentarily in cold water and pouring the water off. This soaking and pouring-off process is repeated three times with fresh, cold water each time.[15]

According to the Bible, blood contains the essence of life, and therefore, before meat can be eaten, the animal's life essence must be returned to the Giver of life. To a gourmet, however, blood contains the flavor and juices of meat, and the purpose of roasting or broiling is not to drain off or burn up the blood, but to sear the surface of the meat and retain as much of the "juices" as possible.

The laws of *kashrut* further specify that the meat cannot be touched by any utensil or cooked in any pot that has ever been used in the preparation of dairy foods. The same prohibitions apply, of course, to the serving vessels and utensils. No butter or milk or cream may be on the table during a meat meal, and a certain number of hours must elapse after the meal is finished before one can eat anything made with dairy products.

On the surface, it would appear that Talmudic law *discourages* the eating of meat by surrounding this act with all sorts of prohibitions and taboos. Paradoxically, it could also be asserted that the dietary laws, like the laws of *shechita*, *facilitated* meat-eating by ritually undoing a moral wrong—the killing of a living creature—with acts of atonement that make the eating of animal flesh fitting—*kasher*—for a holy people, a people who worship a God who has mercy on all that lives.

Over the centuries of practice, *shechita* became a powerful force in the Jewish community, both for good and for ill. On the positive side, *shechita* encouraged Jews to live together. "The Jew desirous of observing his dietary laws requires the services of a *shochet*, and to this end he must make his home in a Jewish settlement."[16] In their travels, traditional Jews likewise congregate at kosher eating places or look for kosher foods.[17]

In various countries of Europe, and in America,[18] the Jewish community employed a *shochet* and, to pay for his services, levied a tax upon all kosher meat and poultry sold in the community. This tax not only paid the salary of the *shochet*, it also paid for inspectors of the butcher shops. The *shechita* tax, in some cases, also supported the community's rabbis, Hebrew school, and ritual bath, and provided funds to assist the poor.

One of the first anti-Semitic laws established in Nazi Germany was the adoption, on April 21, 1933, of an anti-*shechita* law. To enforce it, the Nazi government confiscated all the *shechita* knives that could be found.[19] Before that time, and since, the right of Jews to maintain kosher slaughtering facilities has been a vigilantly defended symbol of the Jewish right of residence in various places.

At times *shechita* and the dietary laws have also been a source of tension among Jews, and a disruptive force within the Jewish community. In the eighteenth century, for example, a controversy raged between the rabbinical and Hasidic communities over exactly how sharp a *shochet*'s knife must be. The Hasidim judged that the knives favored by the rabbis were too heavy and blunt to be practical, and therefore adopted a fine and highly polished blade. The traditionalists—known as Mitnagdim—objected that too sharp a blade was prone to nicking and would render the carcass unkosher. The controversy crossed national borders and even continents. Freedman cites position papers issued in Lithuania, a rabbinical opinion written in Egypt, and bans pronounced in Vilna, Galicia, and elsewhere. In one Polish community any *shochet* who used the kind of knife favored by the Hasidim was placed "in extraordinary excommunication"—"They shall not count toward a quorum in a synagogue; none shall give them lodging; their *shechita* is forbidden; none may transact business with them, marry with them or take part in their burial."[20]

The Hasidim retaliated by setting up their own slaughtering facilities in various towns, harassing rabbis who opposed Hasidic slaughtering methods, and denouncing their pious opponents as people who were "stuffing themselves with *treyfe*."[21]

A more recent and milder difference between the Hasidim and the more traditional Jewish community concerns the promotion of *glatt-kosher* meat. This description is applied to meat of an animal whose viscera are perfectly smooth (*glatt*) and free from any scar, blister, or other evidence of pathology, however thoroughly healed it may be.

After an animal has been slaughtered, the *shochet* examines the carcass to determine whether the animal was in good health. If there is any evidence that the animal was either sick or mutilated, the meat is *treyfe*. But what if there is a healed scar or scab on the lung, or some other indication that the animal was once sick but has since recovered? If the animal has recovered by the time it is slaughtered, the meat is kosher. But recovery from illness is not quite as good as absolute freedom from illness, say the Hasidim. Meat from such animals is prized as *glatt-kosher*.[22] To the observer, this is reminiscent of the laws of Leviticus that admitted only a perfect and unblemished animal for Temple sacrifice.

Controversies over *kashrut* have divided not only the Hasidic and Mitnagdic, or traditional, communities. Conservative Jews have differed with Orthodox Jews on several issues—such as whether swordfish is kosher or not[23] and whether an eating establishment that operates on the Sabbath and holy days can be considered kosher.[24] In the Pittsburgh Platform of 1885, Reform Jews boldly rejected the dietary laws in toto as "entirely foreign to our present mental and spiritual state." The dietary laws were not only rejected but even denounced as "apt to obstruct [rather] than to further modern spiritual elevation."[25] Reconstructionism keeps away from the dietary controversy, taking the position that every congregation and generation must decide on the relevance of the dietary laws to its lifestyle.[26]

More and more of the rabbi's time and energy was given to the study of *shechita* and the dietary laws. About one-fourth of the *Shulchan Aruch*, the Jewish Code of Law, is given over to matters of ritual slaughter, the examination of carcasses to determine whether the animal is kosher, and the laws concerning meat and milk. In some cases, says Rabbi Louis I. Rabinowitz, a rabbinical diploma was granted, in Eastern Europe, after examination *only* on those 103 chapters of the Code![27]

Much of the traditional rabbi's function was to advise and decide on everyday questions of *kashrut*—"A pin found in the gullet of a chicken, meat platters mistakenly used for milk products, etc., etc. I am convinced," Rabbi Rabinowitz concludes, "that without . . . being actively conscious of it, the opposition of . . . rabbis to . . . vegetarianism was simply an instinctive feeling" that vegetarianism would render their expertise obsolete.[28]

Rabinowitz's reference to rabbinical opposition to vegetarianism concerns the claim of Rabbi Chaim Zundel Maccoby, pioneer Jewish vegetarian in turn-of-the-century England. Rabbi Maccoby, known also as the Kamenitzer *maggid*, claimed that he had migrated to England in 1890 because he was a strict vegetarian and the local rabbinate in his Polish hometown "persecuted and hounded him on account of it."[29]

In 1935, Abraham Goldman, a New York chemist dedicated to the advancement of *kashrut*, published and distributed at his own expense 48,000 copies of an information book and directory of kosher foods. The congratulations he received from the Jewish public were matched by censures from the rabbinate, who "objected vigorously to the intrusion of a layman into their official rabbinical domain of responding to *sh'ailos* . . . questions of religious matters.[30] Such incidents suggest that some religious functionaries involved in maintaining *shechita* and the dietary laws have drifted into the role of a vested interest. (If the rabbis objected to Goldman's publication because it contained errors or misleading statements, they would have strengthened their case if they pointed to these errors. Freedman gives the impression that they did not do so.) The rabbis seemed to be arguing that only *they* were sufficiently learned and dedicated to deal with the dietary laws, and that the intrusion of laymen into this area was bound to be misleading.

According to Friedman's U.S. survey, reported in 1961, twenty-eight states have kosher laws, but only New York has a governmental Kosher Law Enforcement Bureau. Established in 1934, the bureau maintains a staff of inspectors "assigned to inspect and investigate all places that process, sell or serve kosher food . . . to protect the consumer of kosher food against fraud and misrepresentation."[31] In New York City alone, sixty inspectors police restaurants, delicatessens, caterers, and food handlers of all sorts for evidence of mislabeling and misrepresentation.

[Inspectors] are taught to recognize when the labels of kosher or *trayfe* meats have been altered, and when metal tags that are placed upon processed meats to identify them as *trayfe* have been switched so that *trayfe* meats are tagged as kosher. A popular ruse practiced by the unscrupulous is to pack a barrel of meats that is being sold as kosher with kosher meats near the top of the barrel, and trayfe meats . . . below them. A host of other established machinations have become known to the inspectors over the years, and now are of little value in attempts to defraud the public. The unscrupulous, however, still try to use them and sometimes manage to find new ways.[32]

Inspection is relatively easy in meat markets and supermarkets, where raw foods are packaged, stamped, labeled, or tagged. An expert can judge from the appearance of a raw fowl whether it has been scalded (*treyfe*) or dry-plucked (kosher). However, where cooked food is sold or served, the problem becomes more complicated. Inspection of the kitchen of a kosher hotel revealed, for example, the use of breading containing milk, for veal cutlets.[33]

Inspection involves not only food consumed in New York, but food mass-processed for national distribution—kosher frozen poultry, for example. Since the economic stakes are so high, and food processors are only human, some may be tempted to cut corners even at the price of violating the dietary laws. Others may innocently and inadvertently be careless, especially since kosher food is often manufactured by non-Jewish firms. In a 1979 publication, Shenker quotes the head of the State Kosher Law Enforcement Bureau, Rabbi Schulem Rubin, as saying: "We're getting in-depth violations that we never got before. . . . The situation is chaotic, without question."[34]

While the state inspector watches over the handling and sale of foods, the *mashgiach* watches over the preparation of kosher foods—in food-processing kitchens, restaurants, catering establishments, even in synagogue kitchens! Rabbi Seymour Freedman describes the pre-union *mashgiach* as a downtrodden, exploited kitchen worker, burdened with menial tasks like peeling potatoes, and often paid—in part, at least—with leftover food and a bottle of liquor. In 1933 Rabbi Chaim Yudel Hurwitch began to organize the Kashruth Supervisors Union, and seven years later his union was awarded a charter by the American Federation of Labor.

With the backing of organized labor—teamsters, musicians, waiters, who would never cross a picket-line wherever Rabbi Hurwitch threw one up—the union had no difficulty finding new and better jobs for its members. Rabbi Freedman observes:

Within the kosher meats and catering industries, many strategic posts are held by union *mashgichim*, giving the organization tremendous power and control over the distribution and sale of kosher meats. There is little doubt that because of this control, Chaim Yudel can stop the flow of kosher meats into the butcher shops of New York City should he desire to do so. The methods employed by Chaim Yudel for achieving such vast power have been criticized by many. But often he has awakened the Jewish community to its responsibilities to observe *kashruth* rather than desecrate the commandments.[35]

Kosher food processing has been called "a billion-dollar business." *Kashrut* supervision is provided by a handful of rabbinic specialists. For example, Rabbi Bernard Levy of O.K. Laboratories supervises the *kashrut* of products like Wesson Oil, Grape Nuts, Maxwell House Coffee, Philadelphia Cream Cheese, and Log Cabin Syrup. Sunkist is also listed as a client of Rabbi Levy. Rabbi Levy's operations require two rabbinical associates, about seventy rabbinical "subcontractors," and an uncounted number of *mashgichim*.[36]

Why do Sunkist products and Maxwell House Coffee need to be certified as kosher? The laws of *kashrut*, it may be argued, are very specific and very detailed, involving all ingredients, even in the most minute quantities, as well as the processing equipment. Undoubtedly, some marketers see the *kashrut* seal as a sales gimmick, something that will give their product a competitive advantage on the supermarket shelf. Rabbi Yacov Lipschutz, representing the Union of Orthodox Jewish Congregations of America, candidly admits: "There are companies who feel that our 'U' symbol would be to their advantage, even though we may feel it's an innocent product. . . . We cannot say to them, 'No, we will not give it to you.' "[37] If coffee can be given a rabbinical label, why not tea? In fact, a tea company hired Rabbi Jacob Cohen to serve as "supervisor" and label its product as kosher for Passover. When asked why *tea* needs to be supervised, Rabbi Cohen responded, "I was wondering about that too."[38]

The laws of *kashrut* have been defended as a means of unifying the people of Israel, but various interest groups have used *kashrut* laws to create tensions and dissensions in the Jewish community. The cost to the Jewish community has not only been moral, it has also been economic. Rabbi Freedman concedes that "the high pricing of kosher meats as compared to non-kosher is a problem which both the religious and civil authorities have been grappling with for many years without a solution." He continues:

> And the demand for some reasonable control of this corrupt situation is heard daily because, in addition to the abuse which such unfair pricing of kosher meats represents, its harm to the Jewish community goes even deeper when it results in discouraging young married people from keeping kosher because of their inability to pay high prices.[39]

The case against present-day *shechita* standards and *kashrut* practices would mention the acceptance of castrated animals as kosher, as well as animals and poultry raised under inhumane factory conditions.

The rule against mutilating animals is clearly spelled out in the Bible, yet capons (castrated chickens) and steers (bulls which have been castrated) are routinely processed by *shochetim*, *mashgichim*, and kosher butchers, on the presumption that the castration was not the work of a Jew, but was done by a skillful non-Jew and that the operation did not touch the animal's intestines.[40]

Routinely, kosher butchers sell milk-fed veal, which is produced with such utter disregard for the calf's *basic* well-being (see Levin, p. 66) that the muzzled ox of the Bible, by comparison, lived in Paradise. *Shochetim* practice their holy art on chickens that have never seen daylight, never had the freedom to walk or peck. And union *mashgichim* carefully supervise the roasting of this poultry. But is it any more kosher, in the sense of being religiously "fit" for Jews, than food served at a restaurant that is open for business on Yom Kippur?

The prophets who denounced the excesses and corruption of the Temple sacrifices—what would they say about modern *kashrut* practice now that Jews have moved from the villages of the Middle East and Europe to the vastness of the United States, and now that *kashrut* supervision is bureaucratically organized and sometimes verges on being a big business? By raising these questions, we do not make a controversial subject of the dietary laws. Conservative and Orthodox Jews, Hasidim and Mitnagdim have debated over the correct implementation of the *kashrut* laws for many years. Rather than weaken the Jewish community, debate and self-examination may be a source of renewal of the Jewish way of life.

The presentation of our conjectures concerning the establishment of *shechita* and the dietary laws, and our survey of its practice over the years, serves another purpose. Realizing that vegetarianism was introduced as an *ascetic cult* in Jewish life, and therefore as a threat to the survival of the Jewish people, makes it easy to understand the bias against vegetarianism that is part of the Jewish tradition. This bias is expressed in the Talmudic saying that "there is no rejoicing without eating meat," and in the advice of the *Shulchan Aruch* that one should celebrate the Sabbath with as much meat and poultry as one can afford.

Shechita, the dietary laws, and the eating of meat have served the Jewish people very well, and in some unexpected ways, over the years. Who would have predicted, in the days of the Talmud, that *shechita* taxes would support Talmud Torahs and ritual baths? But times have changed, and the brand of vegetarianism that mobilized the opposition of the Talmudic rabbis is not the vegetarianism of today.

In the time of Maimonides it may have been very true that "the natural food of man consists of vegetables and of the flesh of animals,"[41] but in our generation, thanks to those nutritionists who are heirs of Maimonides in their dedication to preserving human health, a healthful vegetarianism has become an actuality. Life-affirming and life-enhancing rather than ascetic, this new vegetarianism fulfills more completely the Biblical commandments to nurture human life and to treat with compassion all that lives.

A sizable majority of American Jews do not observe the traditional dietary laws. Even among those who classify themselves as Orthodox, from 25 to 60 percent admit that they do not limit themselves to meat which is kosher.[42] Marshall Sklare introduced the term "nonobservant Orthodox" partly in recognition of this anomaly. Conservative Jews likewise have shown a steady decline in observance of the dietary laws. Great Neck (Long Island), for example, has a *mikveh*, two Orthodox synagogues, two Conservative synagogues, three Reform temples, four bookstores, and a symphony orchestra—but not *one* kosher restaurant (other than delicatessens)![43] Writes Erich Isaac, "In no other area in which restrictions have been imposed on Jews have they been so thoroughly discarded as in the requirements concerning food."[44]

Vegetarianism addresses itself not to the small minority of Jews who keep the traditional dietary laws and find a spiritual satisfaction in doing so, but to the great majority of Jews who are, in the words of Rabbi Hershel Matt, "uncomfortable, embarrassed, and confused" over *kashrut* observance.[45]

Nonobservant Jews who feel uncomfortable because they intuit (correctly!) that the dietary laws convey an important ethical theme, a theme too valuable to abandon, may rediscover the *spirit* of kashrut in vegetarianism.

Vegetarianism, of course, eliminates the need for many of the Jewish food rituals. Does it thereby shrink the Jewish significance of everyday life? No, vegetarianism can enrich Jewish life by infusing it with positive Jewish values.

Vegetarianism expresses compassion for animals, by withdrawing support to a meat industry that raises animals by aversive and cruel factory methods.

Vegetarianism is hygienic. It designates a diet which promotes health and combats degenerative diseases. A vegetarian diet is likely to be high in roughage, low in cholesterol, and free of the hormones and additives that are found in meat products.

Vegetarianism can bring together people who value the Jewish way of life and want to learn from each other how to practice vegetarianism Jewishly, how to glorify the Sabbath and Passover table in a way that is both Jewish and vegetarian.[46]

Vegetarianism allows for a more equitable sharing of the food resources of the world, and thus represents one answer to the complex problem of world hunger. Adopting a food practice that allows for a more widespread distribution of food in our generation and in the future, is in the spirit of the Biblical command, "Thou shalt love thy neighbor as thyself."

7

The Celebration of Life

Are the rules of the Bible and Talmud, in their intended net effect, inhibiting or liberating? Was the list of Mosaic prohibitions and commandments intended to lay a burden upon the Jewish spirit? Could the elaborations and expansions of the law in the Talmud only encumber and narrow Jewish life even further? Perhaps the intent of all these rules, paradoxically, was not to impoverish life but to enrich it, not to deny the pleasures of human existence but to celebrate life's pleasures in a spirit of holiness and thanksgiving.

In our eagerness to embrace the concept of a Judaeo-Christian ethic, we may overlook some enduring differences between what Jews and Christians have traditionally stood for. Christianity came upon the Roman world at a time when the Empire was crumbling. Christianity brought to a world of disorganization and despair a message that suffering purified the soul, that this world counted for very little and was but the antechamber to a glorious heavenly reward.

In Judaism, on the other hand, references to heaven and an afterlife are peripheral to a central concern with life on earth. Eternity is vested in the peoplehood of Israel, not in its individual members. "The earth is the Lord's," and the enjoyment of it, therefore, glorifies God. One increases his knowledge of God by experiencing the many delights He has created for man's enjoyment. This would seem to be the logic behind many Talmudic statements promoting the enjoyment of life's pleasures. For example:

43

It is a sin to abstain from that which the Torah permits.[1]

A man will have to justify himself in heaven as to why he did not eat the foods which he saw.[2]

Rabbi Isaac ben Eliezer had a special menu for every day of the year.[3]

Take and eat, take and drink, for this life which we are going to leave is a marriage feast. If you can afford to, enjoy life, for there is no delight in hell, and death is not slow in coming.[4]

Whoever fasts unduly commits a sin.[5]

One should borrow and eat.[6]

Similarly, the Hasidim talk explicitly about "man using his appetites to serve God": "The very taste of food is a pale reflection of the spiritual force which brings the food into being. Man should be led on by it to contemplate the divine vitality in the food and so to God himself."[7]

It is difficult to find the right words for expressing this point of view because English words that deal with the enjoyment of man's appetites are likely to imply that sensuous enjoyment is the *goal* of life. *Epicurean*, for example, is tied to the philosophy "that the goal of man should be a life of . . . pleasure." *Sensualism*, similarly, is defined as "the system of ethics which holds that the pleasures of the senses constitute the greatest good."[8] In Jewish thought, on the other hand, the enjoyment of human appetites is regarded not as a goal in itself, but as a vehicle for coming closer to God by partaking of His creations.

Health is the bodily condition that enables one to celebrate life, and the Talmud saw in the Bible that life, health, and longevity are described as blessings from God:

And the Lord will take away from thee all sickness.[9]

I am the Lord, that healeth thee.[10]

In the Bible, commandments are repeatedly given for attaining holiness and purity, and for avoiding loathsomeness and abomination. Can these

concepts be directly translated into health and cleanliness, disease and contamination? It is not always clear whether a commandment aims at physical
health or at spiritual purity. Even the sages did not agree.

The twelfth-century sage Maimonides, a towering figure in Jewish
thought, clearly stressed the hygienic aspect of the *kashrut* laws. Forbidden
foods are unhealthy, he wrote.

The meat of forbidden animals is difficult to digest.[11]

The fat of the intestines makes us full, interrupts our digestion, and
produces cold and thick blood; it is more fit for fuel than for human
food.[12]

In the fifteenth century, Yitzhak ben Moshe Arama expressed an opposing view, insisting that to reduce the Torah to a medical book "would
be disgraceful." To him, the dietary laws were significant for their spiritual
value in inhibiting man's brutish appetites and developing his higher poten-
tialities.[13]

In our own times, Rabbi Abraham Isaac Kook chose to favor the
spiritual rather than the hygienic interpretation of the *kashrut* commandments. For example, the Bible prohibits eating the meat of an animal that
died of itself, and it is easy to see this as a health measure. No, argued
Rabbi Kook; this commandment symbolizes a *moral* principle—that the
sick are to be helped to recover, and not left to die and then consumed: "Be
compassionate at least on the unfortunate ones . . . if your heart is insensitive to the healthy and strong."[14]

A third position regarding *kashrut* is that it is an expression of God's
will and must therefore be obeyed by a believing Jew whether the laws appeal to his reason or not. A present-day rabbi puts it this way:

[An observant Jew] may search for reasons and seek rational
explanations for all the observances of *kashrut*, but . . . whether he
knows the reasons [or not] . . . he should continue to have faith in the
Divine Healer, just as one has confidence that the medication prescribed by his physician will be beneficial to him even though he may be
ignorant of the ingredients it contains.[15]

It is interesting to note that even with regard to God's laws which are beyond human understanding. God is described as a Divine Healer, and His laws are described as medication.

Some Biblical passages are simply ambiguous—they can be interpreted to hold out the blessing of individual health and longevity, or they can be interpreted to promise the survival of the Hebrew people if they keep God's commandments. For example, Moses says of God's rules: "And thou shalt keep his statutes . . . that thou mayest prolong thy days upon the land."[16] Of the Torah it is said: "Length of days is in her right hand. . . . She is a tree of life to them that lay hold of her."[17] Similarly, "Ye shall therefore keep my statutes, and mine ordinances, which if a man do, he shall live by them."[18] The Talmudic rabbis preferred to interpret the foregoing passages as promises of longevity and health to those who obeyed God's commandments.

If the Bible is sometimes ambiguous as to whether it is referring to individual health, group survival, spiritual well-being, or physical health, the Talmud is much clearer about its devotion to promoting individual physical health and avoiding disease. Talmudic rules cover every aspect of living—personal cleanliness, cleanliness of surroundings, physical exercise, exposure to sunlight and air, avoidance of physical and emotional stress, and, of course, attention to one's diet over and above compliance with the dietary laws.[19]

A recurrent Talmudic principle is that bodily cleanliness leads to spiritual cleanliness—"purity before God." Physical purity betokens moral purity—"it is not admitted that heart and mind can be pure without cleanliness of the body."[20] Frequent bathing and washing is therefore an important aspect of traditional Jewish life.

The washing of the hands and feet in the morning is more effective than any remedy in the world.[21]

Washing the hands was obligatory both before and after partaking of food, as well as at other times. "Who eats bread without washing his hands is equal to one who cohabits with a prostitute."[22]

The rules concerning the washing of hands before meals occupy a considerable portion of the ceremonial law and minute regulations were prescribed as to the manner of pouring the water, the size of the vessel employed, and the kind of water to be used.[23]

It was forbidden to eat from unclean vessels.

Every married woman was required to bathe after each menstrual period.

Washing the hair was believed to avoid infections which may spread to the eyes and cause blindness.[24]

Concern for personal cleanliness led to rules for the avoidance of contaminated objects and persons. The Talmud cautions against the spread of diseases by flies. The Bible calls for the isolation of sufferers from certain diseases. The Talmud warns that coins should not be placed in the mouth because they may have been touched by persons suffering from contagious diseases.[25] In times of plague, people should stay at home and avoid the society of men.[26] In the Talmud it is recognized that some laws forbidding contact have a ritualistic significance, and some are for the purpose of avoiding dangers to health. The Talmud makes it explicit that "you have to be more careful in cases where danger is involved than in those which involve a mere matter of ritual."[27]

Personal cleanliness includes clean clothing, and clean surroundings, free from dirt, smoke, and dust. The water supply must be pure and plentiful.

Spacious dwellings were urged by the rabbis of the Talmud.[28] Windows should face open places,[29] through which the healing sun could enter.[30] Schools and synagogues should likewise be built with attention to good lighting and air circulation.

The house must be kept clean, whitewashed, swept, sprayed with water, and perfumed.[31] Streets and marketplaces must be kept clean.[32] In Jerusalem streets were swept daily.[33]

One must not reside in a city without a river or fountain.[34]

One must not drink from a stagnant source.[35]

One must see the water he drinks to avoid leeches and worms.[36]

Boiled and warm water was considered best.[37]

In the Talmudic period every citizen was obliged to contribute to the upkeep of the waterworks, and even to take a personal share in the building and repair of them.[38]

Public drinking-water was to be kept away from tanneries, cemeteries, and other sources of contamination.[39]

Urban life in general is considered unhealthful.[40]

Talmudic law requires that environmental health hazards be located outside of town. Included are granaries, threshing places, limekilns, tanneries, cemeteries, pottery kilns, and garbage dumps.[41]

Various mealtime recommendations were made in the belief that they favored good health.

Do not eat unless you are hungry; do not drink unless you are thirsty.[42]

Overeating is dangerous.[43]

Do not eat while standing,[44] or when tightly girdled.[45]

Do not speak while eating.[46]

Early breakfasts were believed to strengthen the body, protect it from heat and cold, from mental dullness, from impotence, from intestinal parasites, and from bad moods.[47]

Rabbi Akiba included in his last will advice to his children on eating an early breakfast.[48]

Mealtimes should follow a regular schedule.[49]

Food should appeal to the eye, for the blind do not enjoy their meals fully, it was observed.[50]

The rabbis warned against eating heavy meals immediately before going to bed.[51]

Until the age of forty a solid diet is preferred; above that age, a soft diet is best.[52]

After the meal it is advisable to take a short walk.[53]

Specific foods were recommended—for good appetite, for good digestion, for specific benefits, and even for wisdom.

Salt was considered a prerequisite at every meal.[54]

Wheat is the best grain for bread-making.[55]

Bread is the staff of life.[56]

Bread, wine, and oil are the pillars of nutrition.[57]

Sweets should always be eaten as a dessert.[58]

Drinking water during the meal regulates the bowels.[59]

Wine is excellent when taken in moderation, but is dangerous in excess. Wine should be sipped slowly. Wine increases the volume of blood.[60]

Goat's milk was considered the best.[61]

Green vegetables increase the appetite. Especially valued were onions and garlic. Radishes were said to aid digestion, asparagus to strengthen the eyes and heart, and to aid digestion, cabbage was said to be nourishing, and bean soup to promote happiness.[62]

On fruits—figs were said to supply energy, dates to relieve constipation, and apples good to combat any disease.[63]

Oil was said to give wisdom.[64]

The rabbis prized mental health as well as physical well-being. Their model of a holy man was not a tormented saint, but a wise and insightful sage. Among various Talmudic interpretations of dreams, Rabbi Jonathan expressed a viewpoint that clearly anticipated the psychoanalytic theory that dreams express the dreamer's unconscious conflicts.

A man is shown in a dream only what is suggested by his own thoughts.[65]

Expressing one's secret troubles or fears was recommended as a relief from worries.[66]

Early marriage was promoted in part for the sake of psychological health.[67]

In matters of health, the Talmud is often surprisingly ahead of its times, and initiated practices which may indeed have spared many Jewish communities from such epidemics as the Black Death.[68] On the other hand, the Talmud includes assertions and recommendations which could not be supported by modern knowledge.

Crying was considered injurious to the eyes and to their vision.[69]

One should not eat eggs laid in the neighborhood of a leper.[70]

Pumpkins are as heavy as lead to digest.[71]

Perspiration is dangerous.[72]

Each person, said the rabbis, bears a responsibility to avoid disease, to fight disease even when it might be seen as a divine punishment, and to avoid common practices which actually endanger health and shorten life.

Premature death is due to carelessness.[73]

Care during early childhood results in a healthy old age.[74]

It does not pay to endanger health for the sake of a brief joy.[75]

Out of every hundred deaths, ninety-nine are caused through willful action on the part of the patient.[76]

Men could have lived healthily through a full span of life if it were not for their improper use of food and drinks.[77]

Today, Jehovah's Witnesses and Christian Scientists demonstrate their faith by accepting death as the price for adhering to religious teachings that conflict with medical practice. The Talmudic rabbis, on the contrary, made it explicit that in case of danger to life, *all laws* (except those against idolatry, adultery, and murder) may be violated.[78]

When life was in danger, all prohibitions against desecration of the Sabbath were removed.[79]

Even if the case appears to be hopeless, all efforts should be made to save a life.[80]

When life was in danger, food prohibitions were to be set aside.[81]

Jeopardizing life is worse than trespassing a religious precept.[82]

Children who were sick or bleeders were not circumcised.[83]

A well-known folk legend tells of a shtetl that was scourged by a plague just before the Day of Atonement. When the survivors huddled together in the synagogue on Yom Kippur, the rabbi looked at their emaciated faces and felt that they could not afford a whole day of abstinence from food and drink. To their confusion and shock, the congregation was urged by their rabbi to go home and eat! eat! eat!

Medical knowledge was, of course, highly prized in a culture which gave such priority to health and life. Medical knowledge was not the secret lore of a profession, but was widely studied as the "wisdom [that] giveth life to them that have it."[84] People were advised to consult a physician even when they were in good health.[85] The third chapter of the Book of Proverbs was interpreted by the Talmudic rabbis as a eulogy of medical knowledge.

My son, forget not my law, but let thine heart keep my commandments; for length of days, and long life, and peace, shall they add to thee. . . . Happy is the man that findeth wisdom, and the man that getteth understanding; for . . . length of days is in her right hand, and in her left hand riches and honor. . . . She is a tree of life to those who lay hold upon her, and all her paths are peace.[86]

One must not reside in a city which is without a physician.[87]

The wide-ranging health observations, some astute, some questionable, were not derived from the Bible, but from direct observation of nature. There is no quarrel between science and religion to one who sees God as the Creator of all things. Then the direct study of nature (if that is what we mean by the scientific method) can only bring one closer to a knowledge of God.

An interesting example of how a rabbi used the method of direct field observation is the story of the Talmudic sage who spent eighteen months living among shepherds to study in detail the physical defects of animals, to better understand what a *shochet* should look for in an animal carcass.[88]

The sages might question devotion to scientific study, according to Leo Levi, when science became an end in itself, when it was considered more important than Torah, or equally as important as Torah. Otherwise, "there was never any question" as to the value of science as such.[89]

The goals of promoting health and preserving life are so important in the Jewish tradition that it becomes, one might say, a Jewish obligation to know something about the present-day medical evidence against meat-eating, and about the health benefits of following an enlightened vegetarian regimen. Does this presume that we are wiser than the sages who encouraged meat-eating? No, the present-day importance of vegetarianism is based on the facts that (1) today's meat supply contains additives and contaminants that were not present at the time of the sages, and (2) today's medical knowledge about saturated fat, cholesterol, heart disease, and colon cancer was not yet revealed at the time when it was said, "There is no rejoicing without meat."

8

What Science Can Tell Us

It is more popular today to think of science as a threat than as a blessing. Can man escape the hazards unleashed by a nuclear technology? Can science escape the stigma that links it to radioactive waste, carcinogenic additives, life-destroying pollution? "Back to nature" has a seductive appeal, as if we could actually retreat from the world that science has shaped, and from the monsters it has spawned.

It does not help to protest against the evil side-effects of science by rejecting everything scientific. We are not saying that the positive side of science outweighs its threat. No, we are only saying that even if we must live in a world threatened by the unwanted by-products of science, let us not ignore scientific findings or insights that can advance our understanding of life, that can improve the quality of life, that point to greater spiritual gratification. We would like to ask, therefore, what can science tell us about the beginnings of human foodways, and about man's future as a vegetarian?

We can see an interesting parallel between the Biblical story of man's origin in the Garden of Eden and the anthropologists' belief that human beginnings took place several million years ago in a tropical rain-forest, a vegetarian paradise abounding with fruits, nuts, and berries. The parallel becomes more remarkable when the story of the expulsion from Eden is compared to the geological evidence that a few million years ago the face of the earth was very gradually reshaped by climatic changes—and the tropical rain-forests, which once covered most of Europe, Asia, and a good part of

Africa, dried out to a very large extent and were transformed into open grasslands suitable not for vegetarian primates but for grazing animals and predators.

As the rain-forests contracted and the prairies expanded, man's forebears evolved from tree dwellers to inhabitants of the open prairie. To ease this transition, there always existed a vast forest edge which was part forest and part prairie. This area served as a place where early man could adapt to his new habitat without abandoning his old one.

It is believed that for about a million years a vegetarian species of early man and a hunting species lived side by side in East Africa. The vegetarian species (*Paranthropus*) did not change over that long period and eventually disappeared. The hunters (*Australopithecus*), on the other hand, evolved rapidly and, over a million years, became larger, more powerful, and brainier. Why? Eye-hand coordination, evolved as a means of swinging from limb to limb through the tropical forests, became an important skill for making and using hunting and meat-eating tools. Hunters range far and wide in search of food. They have to cope with strange surroundings and novel situations. They have to defend themselves with brawn as well as with brain. All these activities seem to have favored the development of intelligence and physique.[1]

How did man's vegetarian forebears acquire a taste for the flesh of grazing animals? Before man became a hunter, perhaps he was first a scavenger, competing with hyenas and jackals for leftovers of animals killed by predators.[2] Gradually, man developed the brain, the brawn, the tools, and the social organization to hunt down his own prey.

Today's joggers exercise skills man evolved from chasing down his prey. But man also bears distinct marks of his still older vegetarian past. The hands that produced and wielded hunting tools were the same hands that managed arboreal locomotion, fruit collecting, berry raking, and root digging. Likewise man retains a vegetarian jaw and teeth—grinding teeth and a lower jaw that moves from side to side for chewing. Carnivorous animals cannot chew; they tear. Their teeth and jaws function like a pair of shears rather than like a mortar and pestle.

Compared with food gathering, hunting not only requires more intelligence and more strength, it also calls for more teamwork. Hunting leads to a greater variety of specialized roles—tool-maker, tool-user, scout, strategist, butcher, fire-maker, husband and wife.[3] It is conjectured that hunting gave rise to man's complex social organization. Hunting may have also introduced man to the enduring moral and religious questions, by posing problems of sharing, and by confronting him with danger and death. No doubt hunting skills were easily extended to the practice of warfare and cannibalism.

In physique, in intelligence, in social organization—it is impossible to know in how many more ways—the human animal was shaped by his hunting past. Vegetarians who regard meat-eating as a detail of human experience, a "mistake" man stumbled into, are wrong. Vegetarians who think they can separate themselves from man's meat-eating past by trading the Hebrew tradition for a vegetarian religion of the East are wrong. From an anthropological standpoint, it is impossible to separate human nature, as we know it, from its hunting origins. Paradoxically, the intelligence we need to use to work out a healthful and satisfying vegetarian regimen is a human talent that evolved from hundreds of thousands of years of hunting!

How did the transition from hunter to herder come about? Baby animals orphaned by the hunt and adopted by the hunters were probably the inadvertent beginnings of the domestication of animals, and about ten thousand years ago man became more of a herder than a hunter.

The domestication of wild animals was followed by the domestication of wild grasses, and man divided his time between herding and tilling the soil. The various grains are, in fact, domesticated forms of wild grasses, varieties that grow shorter and more compact ears. More importantly, in domesticated varieties, the chaff separates more easily from the grain. By roasting, grinding, and cooking it, grain can yield nutlike and tuberlike foods.[4] And the grass stalks that are left over serve nicely as straw for his oxen—bedding and food for the beasts of burden that help till the soil.

Economic pressure, whether it is seen as a scarcity of land or as a growth of population, is bound to favor agriculture over herding. Land put down to grain can feed far more people than the same land devoted to livestock. This is the basic thesis so eloquently championed in Lappe's *Diet for a Small Planet*. Thousands of years before man could read, this fundamental law of economics made itself felt.

Agriculture presented the first possibility for man to once again become a vegetarian, living on "analog fruits and nuts" made from the seeds of domesticated grasses. Grain by itself is a poor nutritional alternative to a meat diet, and anthropologists have been impressed by the physical inferiority of tribal "vegetarians" when compared with tribal meat-eaters.

The people of northwest India, who eat more foods of animal origin than people in other regions of India and have a higher protein intake, are generally healthier, vigorous and well developed; many peoples of the south and east are poorly developed, disease-ridden, and lacking in energy. The pastoral Masai of Kenya, whose diet includes substantial amounts of milk, blood, and flesh, are tall and vigorous, and healthy, whereas their Kikuyu neighbors, who live almost exclusively on millet, maise, sweet potatoes, and yams, are smaller, weaker, and less resistant to certain tropical diseases, as well as to tuberculosis and pneumonia. In fact the average Masai woman is as strong as the average Kikuyu man.[5]

By way of contrast, DeVore and White describe the Himalayan Hunzas as a people of "outstanding health and tremendous vigor" who for practical reasons "are lacto-vegetarians. . . . They have so little arable land, they simply can't afford to raise animals for meat."[6] But more often, field experience leads anthropologists to compare vigorous, well-developed meat-eating tribes with puny and disease-ridden grain-eaters. This has fostered the conclusion that flesh-eating is very good for man and that vegetarianism is a highly questionable, if not dangerous, practice. This kind of thinking led Vilhjalmur Stefansson to champion the all-flesh diet as conducive to robust health, and to ridicule the nutritionists' promotion of "green, leafy vegetables."

Stefansson realized that modern vegetarians cannot be compared with tribal grain-eaters. In his view, modern vegetarians, to a considerable degree, live on "monkey food"—fruits, nuts, berries, roots, and tubers—the kind of food man ate in the tropical forests in which he evolved, before the grasslands developed and man became a hunter of animal flesh.

A grain diet becomes significantly more nutritious when it is combined with legumes—some kind of bean, or peanuts. Taken alone, grain and beans are both nutritionally deficient "incomplete proteins" compared to eggs, meat, or dairy products. But the deficiencies of grains and the deficiencies of legumes differ. Together grains and legumes complement each other, and a grain-bean mixture can become a complete meat replacement—no different from meat from a nutritional standpoint! This is, likewise, a basic theme of *Diet for a Small Planet*, and a principle that was well practiced by many preliterate peoples.

Grain and bean food combinations may be found in traditional foods eaten all over the world. The following list is probably less than complete.

Africa (Tuareg of the Sahara)
   lentil and bulgur wheat stew
   porridge and noodles from garbanzo bean flour and millet[7]

Asia (the Hunzas of the Himalayas)
   barley and garbanzo curry[8]

Europe (Italy)
   pasta with lentils (pasta con lenticchi)
   pasta with beans (pasta e fagioli, or, in Sicilian dialect, pasta-fazoo)

Far East (China and Japan, except for last item)
   green soybeans and rice
   dry soybeans and rice
   bean sprouts and rice
   tofu (soybean curd) and rice
   pea pods and rice
   peanuts and rice
   rice and lentils (India)

Latin America (Mexico)
   rice and beans (arroz y frijoles)
   corn tortillas stuffed with puréed beans (tacos)

Middle East
   hummis (ground chick peas or garbanzos) with pita bread
   lentils with rice (meggadarra)
   wheat bulgur and garbanzos (tabouli)

North America
   chili beans and corn-bread
   succotash (an American Indian corn-and-bean combination)

The nutritional advantage of combining grains and legumes, or of eating grains and legumes separately at the same meal, was correctly intuited by various preliterate peoples, but the privilege of understanding this advantage—what basic foods man requires and how the body uses them—is due to laboratory discoveries in the twentieth century.

Compared with American folk heroes like Luther Burbank and George Washington Carver, William Cumming Rose is absolutely unknown (outside of professional circles), yet it is this University of Illinois biochemist who identified the eight essential amino acids—the cornerstone finding of modern nutrition.[9] Before his time, it was already established that although sugar, fat, or starch could be converted into energy, *protein* was necessary for growth or rebuilding of the body. It was likewise known that there were twenty-two basic compounds—the amino acids—that went into the making of protein substances. It remained for Professor Rose to discover which of these twenty-two amino acids the human body could fabricate by modifying other available amino acids and which were *essential*—that is, had to be eaten regularly if the human body was to grow and repair itself normally. Reported in scholarly journals in the 1940s and 1950s, the identification of the eight essential amino acids (ten for infants) was the significant discovery of William C. Rose.

Using Rose's findings, we can say that meats, eggs, and dairy products are "complete proteins," or "high-quality proteins," because they contain all the essential amino acids. Taken alone, beans and grain are "poor-quality" or "incomplete" protein foods. But the deficiencies of grains and the deficiencies of legumes are not the same, and legumes and grain eaten at the same time provide all the amino acids essential for growth and repair of human tissue. This is the principle of synergism, or complementarity, which is an essential principle of scientific vegetarianism.

Writers on scientific vegetarianism—like Lappé, Sussman, and Robertson—stress two facts about protein complementarity:

1. The nutritionally optimal combination of grain and beans is not 50-50, but closer to 75 percent grain, 25 percent beans.
2. Grain and beans do not have to be cooked together or eaten together, but should be eaten within the same hour to enable the body to use all the essential amino acids as they are needed. (Otherwise, "incomplete" protein may be used as energy or converted into fat.)[10]

Does this mean that a vegetarian must eat grains and legumes at every meal? How dull! Not so dull when you realize that "grain" includes bread, pasta, bulgur, rice, millet, oats, and corn; and that "legumes" include beans of many varieties, lentils, bean sprouts, tofu, green peas, green beans, peanuts and peanut butter. Legumes can be served in soups, as hot vegetables, or as cold vinaigrettes (marinated in salad dressing). Add to the vegetarian diet milk, eggs, cheese, salad vegetables, seeds, and what Stefansson calls the "monkey foods"—nuts, fruits, berries, tubers, shoots—and the vegetarian pantry looks both varied and appetizing. Vegetarianism becomes not a "sacrifice" but a challenge and an invitation to healthy and sane living.

The variety of foods available to the present-day vegetarian in an American city is augmented by a transportation system that ships fresh produce to cities from all parts of the country by air or railroad, and is further augmented by advances in food processing—canning, freezing, vacuum-freezing, freeze-drying, sun-drying.

In 1847, the first Vegetarian Society was founded in Ramsgate, England. Around the end of the century, the Kamenitzer *maggid* began to practice vegetarianism in a Polish *shtetl*. In those days and places, vegetarianism demanded a far more restricted food regimen, and a deeper commitment and greater health risk, than vegetarian practice does today.

What is meant, you may ask, by *scientific* vegetarianism? And is it any closer to the Jewish tradition than any other kind of vegetarianism? Scientific vegetarianism, as I would define it, looks to the medical and scientific community for guidance in making vegetarian practice as healthful and easy as possible.

Not all vegetarians follow this point of view. "Macrobiotics" follow a regimen whose basis is philosophical rather than scientific. One can find advocates of raw foods, of organically-grown foods, and of foods that have fallen to the ground but have not been forcibly detached from the plant. The exponents of each of these practices further restrict the list of "permissible foods" and do not seem to care whether there is scientific support for their principles.

Vegans restrict their diet to foods of plant origin. They do not eat eggs or dairy foods (but may eat honey, which is as completely a product of animal metabolism as milk). Vegans are sometimes regarded as complete or "true" vegetarians, and one can find robust practitioners of veganism. However, the risk of nutritional deficiency is much greater, especially for growing children and pregnant or nursing mothers. The philosophical gains of vegan practice must, therefore, be balanced against these practical costs.

I once met a Swiss-trained chef who would not use lecithin because it is not a "whole food." I talked with a graduate student in nutrition who would not advocate the eating of gluten because it is not a "whole food." Neither of these biases is supported by scientific evidence. Like the organic bias, the macrobiotic bias, and the raw food bias, the whole-food bias is philosophical rather than empirical or scientific. From a Jewish point of view, the enhancement of life and compassion toward animals are a sufficient moral foundation for a food practice. The Jewish tradition has always welcomed scientific guidance. For as *Pirke Aboth* asks and answers, "Who is wise? He who learns from all men."[11]

9

Steps Toward Vegetarianism in Recent Jewish Life

The theme of vegetarianism comes up in Jewish life in a variety of times and places. In 1884, in St. Petersburg, appeared the first modern Jewish writing on vegetarianism, *The Theory of Vegetarianism*, by I. B. Levinsohn. Mention has already been made of the Kamenitzer *maggid*, the Reverend Chaim Zundel Maccoby, who settled in London around 1890 and preached on Torah and vegetarianism in the streets of London. Rabbi Maccoby has been described as a

> great and saintly preacher . . . and a dedicated vegetarian . . . who wore shoes of cloth to show his abhorrence of leather. . . . He brought beauty into the lives of London's East End Jews by teaching them compassion for all living creatures.
> As a deeply religious man, he had a tremendous following. The crowds were such that even the traffic was held up when he preached in the streets.[1]

In 1896, in New York, Aaron H. Frankel wrote a *Torah of Vegetarianism*, subsequently translated into Yiddish and published in a series of four pamphlets. He attempted to organize a Jewish vegetarian society in New York. Four more Yiddish books on vegetarianism were subsequently published—in 1913 *Vegetarianism*, by H. Goldblum; in 1921 *Vegetarianism*, by Elisee Reclus; in 1952 *The Voice of the Vegetarian*, edited by Nathan S. Davis; in 1956 *Shall We Eat Flesh?* by Benzion Liber (the book originally appeared in English in 1934).

Yiddish-language vegetarian cookbooks were published in 1926 (*Rational Eating*, by Mr. and Mrs. A. B. Mishulow) and in 1931 (*Cookbook for Health*, by Lena Brown). Attempts were made to launch Yiddish vegetarian periodicals in Brooklyn, 1921 (*Vegetarian World*), and in Los Angeles, 1929 (*Vegetarian Thought*). A 1977 issue of the *Jewish Vegetarian* carried an article on Jewish vegetarianism in the United States and named a 300-member North American Vegetarian Society headed by Jonathan Wolf.[2] The *Vegetarian Times* of June 1980 lists a Jewish Vegetarian Society in Forest Hills, N.Y., and a Jewish Vegetarian Society of Maryland, in Baltimore City.

In Israel today vegetarianism is an active movement, as it was in Mandatory Palestine, before the advent of statehood. Kibbutz Gezer, in the Judean foothills, is described as an enterprise of "young vegetarians, all idealists." Amirim, in eastern Upper Galilee, is a vegetarian *moshav*. An article on "Vegetarian Israel" mentions two organizations—the Israel Vegetarian Movement (or Union) and the Haifa Vegetarian Society.[3] It is estimated that there are about 80,000 vegetarians in Israel—nearly 4 percent of the population.[4]

In 1938, a Polish Jewish publisher, Kletzkin, issued a Yiddish vegetarian cookbook authored by Fania Levando, who operated a Jewish vegetarian restaurant in the city of Vilna, Poland (now the capital of Lithuania). Called Kuchina Dieta-Jarska, the author's restaurant was a gathering place for Yiddish artists and writers, whose testimonials are included at the end of the book. In 235 pages were listed 400 vegetarian adaptations of traditional Jewish foods. The author's introduction shows a sensitivity to both the hygienic and ethical aspects of vegetarianism.

> The greatest medical authorities have long established that dishes of fruits and vegetables are much healthier . . . than meat dishes. . . . There is hardly a household without one or more members of the family suffering from some ailment which forbids them to eat meat and makes them keep to a diet. There is also the humanitarian aspect, which finds expression in the vegetarian movement, not to kill any living creature.
>
> So I have decided to publish this first Yiddish vegetarian cookery book.[5]

In the 1960s, Miss Vivien Pick wrote a letter to the *London Jewish*

Chronicle, inviting interested readers to join a small circle of Jewish vegetarians meeting in the London area. So unexpectedly great was the response that Vivien, then attending the Royal College of Music, asked her father to handle the correspondence that continued to flow from her letter. Out of this serendipity, Vivien's father, Philip L. Pick, himself a second-generation vegetarian, has built the Jewish Vegetarian Society, an international organization which publishes the quarterly *Jewish Vegetarian* and has become a significant factor in the world vegetarian movement.

In an article in the *National Jewish Monthly* in 1976, Arlene Groner observes an increase in "interest in vegetarianism . . . at northeastern colleges with large Jewish populations. . . . For the last three years, one-third of the thirty-five residents at Kibbutz Langdon, a *havura* in Madison, Wisconsin, have been vegetarians. The Hillel House of Southern Illinois University at Carbondale, runs a vegetarian restaurant. In 1974, a cook was hired by Camp Ramah in Palmer, Massachusetts, to provide a special diet for the camp's vegetarians."[6]

A number of public figures in recent Jewish life have chosen and supported the vegetarian way of life. The first Ashkenazi Chief Rabbi of Israel, the late Abraham Isaac Kook, wrote an essay entitled "A Vision of Vegetarianism and Peace," which is quoted in several places in this book. The present Ashkenazi Chief Rabbi of Israel, Rabbi Shlomo Goren, is likewise a vegetarian. "The Rabbi's wife is a lifelong vegetarian, having been raised in an Orthodox vegetarian household in Jerusalem. The Rabbi himself became a vegetarian, reportedly, after supervising the Army's slaughterhouses!"[7]

Two Jewish winners of the Nobel Prize for literature, S. Y. Agnon and Isaac Bashevis Singer, are practicing vegetarians, and both have woven the theme of vegetarianism into their stories. Agnon describes the Sabbath observance of a saintly old couple:

> He received the Sabbath with sweet song and chanted the hallowing tunefully over raisin wine; while it was still day and the sun came to gaze at his glass. . . . The table was well spread with all manner of fruit, beans, greenstuffs and good pies, plum water tasting like wine, but of flesh and fish there was never a sign. . . . In truth it is in no way obligatory to eat flesh and fish. . . . The old man and his wife had never tasted flesh since growing to maturity.
> . . . That old man was one of the Thirty-six Hidden Saints upon

whom the whole world rests, and can therefore be presumed to have known what is acceptable to Him, may He be blessed.[8]

In *The Manor*, Isaac Bashevis Singer expresses his sentiments about animal slaughter through the thoughts of Jochanan.

> There was a run on roosters, sacrificed before the [Yom Kippur] holiday for the redemption of sins. . . . Early on the morning before Yom Kippur, the rabbi and his family gathered to offer the sacrifice. . . . The men held the roosters by the feet and swung them overhead; the women did the same with hens. This sacrifice, which ended with the eating of the chickens, always caused Jochanan anguish. . . . It disturbed Jochanan to take a fowl by its claws and feel its body trembling. Although birds committed no acts of piety, neither did they sin. Who could say that he, Jochanan, was more worthy to live than the creature sacrificed for him? . . . Jochanan stood nearby [the *shochet*], his head lowered, his face pale, remembering the story of Cain and Abel as well as the words, "And the preeminence of man over the beast is naught."[9]

Elsewhere Singer comments autobiographically on his vegetarian experience.

> Early in my life I came to the conclusion that there was no basic difference between man and animals. If a man has the heart to cut the throat of a chicken or a calf, there's no reason he should not be willing to cut the throat of a man.
>
> It took me a long time to come to the decision to be a vegetarian because I was always afraid I'd starve to death. But never did I have a moment in these 15 years when I regretted that decision.[10]

10

Eight Questions and Answers

1. A rabbi expresses a traditional Jewish attitude toward vegetarianism in the following words: "For a Jew to adopt vegetarianism because he objects to killing animals for food is to introduce a moral and theological idea which suggests that Judaism has, in fact, been wrong all the time in not advocating vegetarianism."[1] How do you answer that?

The sages agree that man was created as a vegetarian, and it is prophesied that in the time of the Messiah man will return to vegetarianism ("The lion will eat straw like the ox"). In the Bible therefore, it may be said, vegetarianism is held up as an ideal, even though the Jews were permitted to slaughter grazing (vegetarian!) animals in prescribed ways because man seemed to have an unquenchable craving for meat. The Temple sacrifice system may be regarded, in part, as an act of atonement for violating God's rule of compassion for all living things.

Our times differ from the days of the Bible, and some of these differences raise the question as to whether we still need this permission to slaughter animals. Modern biochemistry tells us how to satisfy man's nutritional needs completely without the use of meat, so that the physiological craving for meat is no longer a problem. Modern medicine tells us with increasing clarity that meat-eating does not favor the preservation of life. Vegetarianism points toward a solution to the world hunger problem, a phenomenon of our times which the Biblical ethic cannot let us ignore.

In a world of change, Judaism may *have* to change in order to be true to its traditional values. But Judaism has not "been wrong all the time" any more than the findings of biochemistry have been known all the time, or that meat has contained questionable additives and contaminants all the time.

2. What if everyone was vegetarian?

Vegetarianism is for those who find a spiritual satisfaction in "not eating things that breathe." Not everyone feels this way, and that's all right. Vegetarianism is *one* way to observe Jewish values, but there are many other ways: through rabbinical study, through Hasidic dancing, through prayer, through fund-raising, through working on a *kibbutz*. And these ways are not mutually exclusive. They allow different people to celebrate Judaism in different ways, and in more ways than one.

An appreciation of individual differences has deep roots in Jewish thought. In the stories of Cain and Abel, Joseph and Esau, and Moses and Aaron, the Bible shows us brothers whose differences are striking, though they were born to the same parents and raised in the same home. The Passover Haggadah recognizes that to teach one's children about the flight from Egypt, one must adapt the story to the wise son, the evil son, the simple son, and to the one who is even "too simple to inquire."

In his *Code of Law and Ethics*, Maimonides recognizes that individual variation is a fundamental law of life.

One man is hot-tempered, constantly angry; another is self-possessed and never angry, or only slightly and rarely so. One man is excessively proud; another is excessively meek. One man indulges his appetites without being sufficiently gratified; another is pure of heart and does not crave even the few essentials that the body requires. . . . And so it is with all human dispositions, such as hilarity and gloom, niggardliness and generosity, cruelty and compassion, cowardice and courage.[2]

Motives for or against vegetarianism vary from person to person. For some, the health motive is all-important. It is popular to look down on "health faddists," but in the Jewish tradition, the preservation of life has a high ethical value. ("Mortifying the flesh to purify the soul" is not a Jewish idea.)

Vegetarianism probably fits the nutritional needs of some people more easily than others. This conjecture is suggested by the research and writings of Roger J. Williams, who places great emphasis on individual differences in nutritional needs.[3] Whether the question is to determine how much protein a person needs per day or the extent of one's daily need for vitamins, minerals, calories, or trace elements, Williams insists that what might be adequate for one person could be called a deprivation for another. Adjustment to a vegetarian diet would undoubtedly be easier for some than for others—psychologically and even physically.

For whatever reason, appetites vary. "One man's meat is another man's poison." Roger Williams insists this adage deserves to be taken quite seriously.[4] Some people undoubtedly find the practice of vegetarianism easy to adopt, others would feel quite deprived to give up meat-eating.

It is interesting to note that among Seventh-Day Adventists, who have long advocated vegetarianism as a spiritually meaningful regimen, the practice remains quite voluntary. Within an Adventist congregation, some members are practicing vegetarians and others are not. Vegetarianism has a place in a pluralistic society—a society of Protestants, Catholics, Jews, Buddhists, nonbelievers, and so on. What for me is a small concession, an easy adjustment to make, may give great psychological discomfort, or even pain, to someone else. I once came across the statement, "It is easier for a person to change his religion than his eating habits." Yet there are always some people who *do* change their religion, and are glad they made the change. "Converting" to vegetarianism can similarly meet one's *own* spiritual needs, regardless of what foodways are followed by the great majority.

3. I get the impression that vegetarianism is a reentry tactic for disaffected Jews who are looking for new ways to express Jewish values, for Jews who feel they cannot observe the traditional *kashrut*, for example, and want a substitute for it. Am I correct?

You are partially right. Vegetarianism does appeal to what Hasidism calls *dos pintele Yid*, the bit of Jewish sentiment that continues to seek expression after the traditional forms of Jewish practice have been abandoned.

It is a thesis of this book that vegetarianism is *not* a second-rate substitute for *kashrut*, but—in the light of present-day medical knowledge and meat-production practices—that vegetarianism is a valid modern expression of the spirit of *kashrut*.

Groner tells of how Rabbi Everett Gendler and his wife studied Talmudic attitudes toward animals and came to "the conclusion that vegetarianism was the logical next step after *kashrut*—the proper extension of the laws against cruelty to animals."[5] Groner also quotes a rabbinical student who says of adopting a vegetarian regimen, "Now I feel I have achieved the ultimate state of *kashrut*."[6] Surveying halachic vegetarianism for her *National Jewish Monthly* article, Groner was impressed that for all the vegetarian Jews she interviewed, "vegetarianism led to a broader—and, in some cases, deeper—understanding of Judaism . . . the heritage of their fathers."[7]

4. You say that vegetarianism makes a symbolic gesture of concern for the hungry peoples of the world, that vegetarianism expresses a willingness to share more equitably in the world's limited food resources. Does vegetarian practice ever come close to actually helping the world's hungry?

According to Robertson and her co-authors, a reduction in demand for meat has on occasion actually released more grain to the poorer countries.

As of mid-1975, world famine has intensified to the point that fifteen thousand human beings, most of them children, are dying of malnutrition each day. . . . Meanwhile . . . the major health problems in the United States continue to be those related to overconsumption. . . . We now consume about twice the protein our bodies need, and beef is our hands-down favorite way of doing it. . . . Every pound of beef on our table represents sixteen pounds of grains and legumes removed from the total available to a hungry world. What we do not realize is that this high-protein feed is administered to a steer during the last few weeks of its existence. The sole function of most of the soybeans and other feed crops we raise is to turn lean range-fed beef into the marbled-fat beef that our doctors warn us against.

The relationship between meat consumption and available grain is therefore more sensitive than we might think. . . . In 1974, when the market for meat did fall, the grain that was so unexpectedly released actually *did* find its way to poorer countries.[8]

The needs of the hungry people of the world are too great to depend on direct benefits to them from vegetarian practice. Rather let us use vegetarianism as a daily reminder that 500 million people in the world *are* hungry or even starving, and make it our duty to find ways to alleviate their plight.

5. There are moments when you come dangerously close to self-righteousness, and sound as if all vegetarians are good and all non-vegetarians are bad. You are probably a vegetarian for good reasons, but some people become vegetarian for trivial or even pathological reasons, wouldn't you agree?

Rabbi Kook anticipated your question by acknowledging that there are indeed false motives for vegetarian practice.

Vegetarianism may allow the wicked to appease their conscience and flatter their ego by performing acts of kindness toward animals while they behave like criminals and oppressors toward other people! It is easy for a wicked person to be kind to animals. Animals do not arouse a person's enmity and envy. Let us not underestimate man's capacity for finding ways to escape his moral responsibility. Man's first responsibility is to man; and the fulfillment of the moral task is still very incomplete. When humanity approaches its full potential, then and only then can man and animals live in peace.[9]

The doors to vegetarian practice are open, and attract a wide variety of adherents. As a practicing vegetarian, your spiritual companions will include Rabbi Abraham Isaac Kook, A. D. Gordon, spiritual mentor of the Zionist labor movement, the Reverend Maccoby, Franz Kafka, I. L. Peretz, S. Y. Agnon, and Isaac Bashevis Singer, and your social companions are likely to include as high a proportion of persons of excellent character as any church, synagogue, college faculty, or other social group.

6. To me, an important part of Jewishness is the preservation of *tradition*—serving the same foods our grandparents ate, observing the same dietary laws they followed. The world around us is changing so rapidly—can you blame me for wanting to cherish a few traditions?

Because the world *is* changing so rapidly, the meats your ancestors ate are not really the meats you get today—complete with the additives and contaminants you'd rather not have. Animals and poultry are not raised today like farm creatures were raised a generation ago. Today, you buy the products of meat-factories where animals are subjected to conditions that make their meat kosher in name only.

The constancy of Jewish practice over the generations and over the world is more of an illusion than a fact. Today a couple sit side-by-side in a Conservative synagogue. The man does not wear a beard, and his wife does not wear a wig. This sight would have disturbed their parents and scandalized their grandparents. Seventy-five years ago those who went to Palestine were regarded as social misfits and radicals. Today those who "make *aliyah*" can count on the moral support and admiration of friends and family. Traditionally, chicken was *pareve* in Holland and *fleishig* in most other places.

Continuity and change are both part of life, and both are characteristic of Jewish life. Moreover, change may even *serve* the process of continuity. Do not the advocates of Reform Judaism claim that their style of Jewish practice provide ties for thousands who, for whatever reasons, could not identify with the traditional forms of Judaism?

Jewish vegetarianism is an expression of radical traditionalism. It holds that what is most worth preserving in Jewish life are its values—compassion for all that lives, concern for health and life, and regard for the welfare of those who live in want. *These* are the traditions most worth cherishing, even more dearly than chicken soup and roast brisket.

7. Your presentation of Jewish vegetarianism makes constant reference to the Bible and to God. Wouldn't it be simpler to present the vegetarian argument in secular terms? Aren't many vegetarians agnostics or even atheists?

To many people, vegetarianism has a spiritual as well as a practical meaning. Some turn to the Eastern religions and their ideas of karma and reincarnation to relate vegetarian practice to spiritual values. A goal of this book is to show how vegetarianism is related to the Jewish tradition, and that goal called for references to the Bible, the Talmud, and rabbinical thought. In these sources, God is a recurrent and pervasive concept.

In the Jewish tradition as in other religions, the word *God* represents the concept of an inner power, an ennobling power, a universal power, a transcendent power, and an invisible power.[10] In some theological traditions it is important to say whether that power is supernatural or not. In the Jewish tradition it is also important, but it is not universally important.

The idea that God means whatever you think God means may shock and trouble many Christian theologians, but it is not at all disturbing to Jewish thinkers, who for centuries have characterized God as "hidden" or "unknowable." Jacob B. Agus writes that "some historians have even assumed that the Jewish people lacked the capacity to feel the grandeur of the mystic's endeavor to sense the immediate presence of the Divine Being . . . because the Jewish religion stressed exclusively the transcendence and incomprehensibility of the Diety."[11] When asked to describe his conception of God, Elie Wiesel recalled the words of Kafka: " 'Man cannot speak *of* God. If, at all, he can speak *to* God.' So I am still trying to speak *to* Him. How can we speak *of* Him?"[12]

For many years, the Reconstructionist movement has made the humanist idea of God part of its explicit platform. Reconstructionist rabbis serve both Conservative and Reform congregations.

In one of his novels, Isaac Bashevis Singer expresses a pious Jew's reconciliation to the nonexistence of a supernatural God: "Even if death should prove him wrong. If he should face an end without Judgement or Judge, he will have lived . . . according to his convictions and his taste."[13]

8. You regard vegetarianism as a food ritual that partakes of the spirit of *kashrut*. In anthropology, we learn about the rituals of tribal and traditional groups, but does ritual still have a place in a scientifically informed society?

When you say hello or goodbye, you are observing a ritual. When you observe a birthday or an anniversary, you are observing a ritual. The psychology of ritual is an almost unwritten chapter.[14]

Sigmund Freud is not considered a defender of the Jewish tradition. He was a radical thinker, and had a deep attachment to nineteenth-century rationalism. Still, he remained a Jew, and he spoke and wrote in positive terms about his Jewish identity.[15] Freud makes two positive statements about religious ritual. In *The Future of an Illusion* Freud acknowledges that religious ritual may help "devout believers" cope with anxiety "without taking flight to neurotic symptoms."[16] In "Obsessive Acts and Religious Practices," Freud observes that neurotic motives tend to encumber religious rituals with petty details, and this tendency requires occasional reforms aimed "at the re-establishment of the original relative values."[17] Was Freud thinking about the Jewish dietary laws?

Rabbi Richard Rubenstein has advanced the psychologically stimulating idea that a nonverbal ritual—because it is so unstructured—is particularly suitable for expressing and projecting "our unconscious [fears and wishes] concerning the dilemmas of existence." Ritual becomes indispenable for sharing and celebrating "the decisive moments of existence . . . at both the conscious and unconscious levels."[18] Ritual permits the expression of sentiments which cannot be readily put into words. Ritual can be a unifying force. It permits the sharing of a practice which may have different unconscious meanings to different people.

Dare we look for sacred moments in modern life? Martin Buber proposed that we seek sacred moments in our everyday relations with other people. The *kashrut* tradition similarly imbues the everyday act of eating with holiness. Food shopping, meal planning, food preparation, and eating take on a spiritual dimension. By adopting vegetarianism, Jews who would feel burdened or resentful if they were forced to practice the traditional *kashrut* might share something of the spiritual experience of those Jews who can practice the traditional *kashrut* wholeheartedly and sincerely.[19]

Buber recalls a Hasidic myth that when God created the world, holy sparks (*nizozot*) were released, that are now imprisoned in everyday objects of all kinds. When everyday objects are used in a spirit of holiness, said the Baal Shem, founder of Hasidism, these holy sparks are once more released. "Eating can be holier than fasting," writes Buber.[20]

Can eating be indeed holier than fasting, or, at least, can eating be made more compassionate, more healthful, and more humane, and can this be done in a spirit of celebration rather than asceticism? Jewish vegetarianism is an approach to this goal.

Appendix I

What's Cooking?

Discussions of vegetarianism often begin on a lofty philosophical plane and eventually lead to an exchange of recipes, how to make cottage cheese, or how to grow alfalfa sprouts. Similarly, I would like to share with the reader some of several years' experience in vegetarian cooking. A caveat is in order—food preferences are a very personal matter. What may seem important or worthwhile to me may be of very little interest to you. This is not a recipe book, though I will include a few recipes, and show you where you can find more recipes I can recommend.

Meat is a relatively concentrated source of flavor, protein, minerals, and vitamins. If you have decided to eliminate meat from your diet, choose your foods with more care for their nutritional value. For example, whole wheat bread is more nutritious than white bread, brown rice is more nutritious than white rice, blackstrap molasses and honey are both more nutritious than refined cane sugar,[1] yogurt and stewed fruit make a more nutritious snack than ready-mix pudding. Look for whole wheat graham crackers at a health food store, get whole wheat flour at a natural foods store, and ask for whole wheat matzos wherever you buy matzos.

If you try to make a "vegetarian version" of a favorite stew or casserole you used to make with chunks of meat or chicken, and slyly try to eliminate the meat or chicken, the results may be less than successful. You'll discover that the meat not only contributed texture, color, and protein, it also contributed flavor and fat. You can successfully vegetarianize some of your favorite recipes by using the following suggestions.

1. Add body to the recipe by adding one or several tablespoons of oil. Try peanut oil or olive oil as an alternative to your usual cooking oil. (For health's sake, don't use solid fats!) Important—a small amount of liquid lecithin (obtainable at health food or natural food stores), maybe one-quarter of a teaspoonful, will make it easy to blend the oil into a sauce, soup, or gravy, so that the result is a uniformly creamy blend, rather than a runny mixture with blobs of oil floating on top![2]

Various anthropologists have observed that peoples whose diet does not include refined sugar show an occasional craving for fat similar to our "sweet tooth."[3] Fat is a regular dietary need. The meat-eater's problem typically is how to reduce his fat intake, but the vegetarian must remember to introduce fat into his (or her) cooking for the sake of good nutrition and satisfying taste.

In American recipes, oil is specified to accomplish something—to sauté, to fry, to shorten. A Chinese cookbook introduced me to the idea of using oil to give flavor and texture to food.

2. Add flavor to your recipes to replace some of the meaty flavor you and your family are accustomed to. Throwing in a few chunks of meat is an easy way to add flavor to a stew, soup, or casserole, but there are various ways to add subtle, interesting aroma to vegetarian dishes. Consider these:

a. Highly flavored vegetables like onions and garlic. Use them with restraint and subtlety. Experiment with the difference between onions sautéed until they are transparent and yellow, and onions that have been sautéed until they are carmelized (but not burnt). Green onions have a place in cooking, not just in salads. (I chop up some of the tops—the part some people discard!—and use it like parsley.) If you're putting a food mixture through a blender, add a clove of fresh garlic, and in a minute it will be thoroughly blended into the mixture. You'll find garlic powder more potent and flavorful than garlic salt.

b. Flavor concentrates like vegetable bouillon cubes, bouillon granules, or hydrolized yeast products like Maggi's Marmite, or Loma Linda Savorex. I have enjoyed using vegetable bouillon cubes imported from Israel, and vegetable bouillon granules blended to approximate beef and chicken flavor. When I'm using a cube, I like to reduce it to a powder to blend it into the soup or sauce right away. For this purpose I keep a small glass mortar and pestle handy. (I also find a mortar and pestle handy to pulverize onion flakes or dried herbs.)

c. Herbs and spices. Learn which combinations work best for you—like oregano, basil, and garlic for Italian flavoring, oregano and dill for Greek flavoring. I found that most chili recipes produced too highly spiced a dish for my taste. I cut the chili powder in half, added more cumin and garlic, and the result was a definite improvement.

Practice subtlety—a dash of Tabasco sauce in a soup or omelette can make it taste "interesting," though not enough has been added to give the food the taste of hot peppers.

Principles (1) and (2) above have to be practiced together. For example, I am sure that some herbs and spices would taste harsh in a watery sauce. Some cooks try to combat the harshness of a vegetarian tomato sauce, for example, by adding sugar. Don't! Mellow it by adding some oil blended with lecithin. A few tablespoons of oil and a little lecithin, added to a can of tomato paste and a can of water, sautéed onions, minced garlic, diced sweet pepper and celery, oregano, basil, and paprika, can be happily blended into a savory topping for spaghetti or cheese ravioli.

Watery, overspiced foods give vegetarianism a bad name! Can you make a mellow, hearty soup without beef stock and soup bones? You sure can. I like a thick soup, and here are some ideas on how to thicken soups without flour.

1. Bake a whole eggplant. Then cut it open, scrape out everything except the outer peel, put the eggplant meat into your blender with enough water to reduce the eggplant to a purée. In another pot I have a mixture of vegetables cooking (diced carrots, shredded cabbage, tomatoes, peas, okra), and when the vegetables are tender, I add the puréed eggplant, oil, lecithin, and flavoring ingredients.

2. Add okra to your soup mixture—as I indicated above. You'll find cut okra among the frozen vegetables. It's a traditional Creole vegetable (also called gumbo) used for thickening soups and stews, and it's worth getting to know.

3. Gumbo filé (the latter word pronounced like filet mignon) is another Creole soup and stew thickener. Actually it is the powdered leaf of the sassafras plant, taken by the Creoles from American Indian cookery. Its flavor is so subtle that you can add a teaspoonful of gumbo filé to a stew or soup and not taste the difference, though it will thicken it. One note of caution—add the powder *after* the stew or soup has been cooked. You can

keep it at serving temperature for a while, but if you cook gumbo filé for any length of time, it makes the dish stringy.⁴

4. I use lentils, beans, or split peas as a soup base. I soak them overnight and cook them until they are tender, then reduce them to a purée in my blender. In ordinary cooking, lentils, beans, or split peas may be cooked with a soup bone for hours so that all the flavor can be extracted from the bone. In the meantime, the legumes are reduced to a purée. But in vegetarian cooking, there's no point to cooking legumes after they're tender. I save time and energy by blending the cooked legumes (with a clove of garlic) to a purée, and then add more vegetables (already cooked, along with the water they cooked in), oil, lecithin, and flavor to taste. Sometimes I only purée about two-thirds of the beans and pour the other third back into the soup to mingle with the vegetables.

A soup doesn't *have* to be thick to be enjoyable. For the sake of sentiment and eating pleasure both, I sometimes make a mock chicken soup. In water in which I have boiled some carrots, celery tops, and onion, I dissolve some chicken-style vegetable bouillon. Strain the soup, dice the carrots and return them to the soup. Blend in a few tablespoons of oil, a drop of lecithin, some garlic powder, a little dill (maybe a half-teaspoonful). Serve it with matzo balls and, as Harry Golden would say, Enjoy! Enjoy!

On the subject of matzo balls, let me pass along an old family tactic. Mix the batter the night before and let it stand in the refrigerator overnight. (Follow the recipe on the matzo meal package.) You'll be surprised how much the mixture will thicken. Try adding a little more water before shaping them and dropping them into boiling water.

I don't apologize for sometimes making vegetarian foods that resemble meat dishes. I think "analog foods" can have appetizing tastes and textures, bring back pleasant memories, and can be enjoyable in every way. Let me say a word about several food items used in "analog cooking."

1. Texturized vegetable protein, a soybean product known as TVP and sold in dry granules and chunks. Printed instructions usually advise to rehydrate with hot water and "use like hamburger." Remember that hamburger is maybe 15 percent fat, and that's what makes it juicy and flavorful. What does TVP taste like after you rehydrate it? Poor and sandy. But mix it with some egg replacement (or oil plus that drop of lecithin), minced onion, and green pepper, and brown the mixture like hash (but don't let it dry out)—and it's just right to eat as hash, to add to chili, or to add to tomato sauce.

In addition to the granular kind of TVP, of which there are several brands, I enjoy a health food store item called Loma Linda Vita-Burger Chunks, a dehydrated product that looks like stewing beef and has a good flavor. Whichever brand you use, whatever recipe you follow, add oil and lecithin (or egg replacement) to make it tasty.

2. Gluten or wheat protein. Gluten is the substance that gives wheat flour its springiness and cohesiveness, and—separated from wheat starch—it is a high-quality protein. Gluten is made from a batch of well-kneaded dough that has been permitted to stand and then is kneaded under water with repeated changes of the water as it becomes cloudy, until most of the starch has been washed out. You then have a mass so rubbery and cohesive it must be run through a grinder to mix it with oil, lecithin, and flavorings, ready for the oven. (For more complete instructions, see Doltzer's *Farm Vegetarian Cookbook*, or Herdt's *Nitty Gritty Foodbook*.)

Instructions for making and using gluten are also contained in Gary Lee's *Chinese Vegetarian Cookbook*. I first learned about gluten from a Chinese student of mine who told me that in China, vegetarian Buddhist monks use mock duck as a dietary mainstay. He wrote out the words for mock duck in Chinese *mun chai ya* 悶齋鴨 and suggested I get a can at a Chinese grocery store.

I was delighted with the discovery, and used mock duck in slices or shreds to add texture interest to salads, soups, fried rice, stir-fry vegetables, and egg roll filling. Slices of mock duck can also be pan-fried. First, dip each slice in a raw egg mixture, then in breadcrumbs (or matzo meal), again in egg, and once more in breadcrumbs. Fry till golden brown. It makes an interesting addition to a mixed grill. Remember, mock duck has the looks and texture of meat, but it's a wheat product and, like all grains, should be part of a meal that includes beans, eggs, milk, or cheese.

After it has been roasted and cooled, gluten can be sliced ever-so-thin, and can be eaten hot or cold. Gluten (or "wheat protein," as the label says) is also the basic ingredient of the canned vegetarian meat analogs for sale at health food stores. Made to look and taste like chicken, ham, or beef, these items are more expensive than Chinese mock duck, and I like the Chinese product better. It's a matter of taste.

"Vegetarian chopped liver" is a popular Jewish delicacy. Here are three variations.[5]

Recipe No. 1	Recipe No. 2	Recipe No. 3
1 large onion diced	1 onion sliced	1½ lb. mushrooms
4 tablespoons oil	2 hard-boiled eggs	½ cup diced onions
salt and pepper	½ cup walnuts	1 hard-boiled egg
1 medium eggplant	1 teaspoon salt	1½ teaspoons salt
diced	¼ teaspoon pepper	½ teaspoon pepper
1 hard-boiled egg		

Sauté onion in oil. Add eggplant and seasonings. Fry until brown. Add chopped egg. Serve hot.	Sauté onion in oil for 15 minutes. Put all ingredients in chopping bowl and chop until very fine. Chill.	Slice mushrooms, combine with onions and cook over medium heat for 10 minutes. Add hard-boiled egg, seasonings, and chop until smooth. Chill.

Don't let vegetarianism lead you or your family to eat too many egg yolks. The cholesterol level of egg yolks is very high, and Dr. Jean Mayer recommends that adults limit their intake to two per week! It's careless to say that eggs are high in cholesterol—it's the *yolk* that contains all the cholesterol. The whites consist of very good protein, water and practically nothing else.

Commercial egg replacements (like Fleischmann's Egg Beaters and Second Nature) are practically all egg white, plus flavoring, coloring, thickeners, and preservatives. After some experimenting, I worked out an egg-replacement recipe of my own, using powdered egg white (though you could, of course, use fresh egg whites). Here's my recipe for a generous two-egg replacement, using either fresh egg whites or powdered egg white.

No-cholesterol egg replacement, using fresh egg whites

Dry ingredients
1 tablespoon dry skim milk
1 tablespoon starch (tapioca starch, potato starch, or corn starch)

Liquid ingredients
2 tablespoons cooking oil
2 egg whites
1 glob liquid lecithin (about the size of a pea is enough)
1½ liquid ounces water

Use a jar that has a tight cover. Add dry ingredients, cover jar, and shake. Add liquid ingredients and seasonings. Cover jar and shake well.

No-cholesterol egg replacement, using powdered egg whites

Dry ingredients	*Liquid ingredients*
1 tablespoon dry skim milk	2 tablespoons cooking oil
1 tablespoon starch (same as above)	1 glob liquid lecithin (same as above)
4 teaspoons egg white powder	3 liquid ounces water

Proceed the same as above. In this recipe it is even more important to mix the dry ingredients thoroughly before adding liquids, to prevent clumping of dry ingredients.

Seasonings are a matter of taste, of course. Try a drop of Tabasco sauce, Savorex, or salt, pepper, and garlic. Better yet, add Cheddar or Muenster cheese, sautéed onions, or sautéed mushrooms—if you plan to make an omelette. The above recipe will give a bland, custardlike approximation of an egg. The only thing that really tastes like a fresh whole egg is a fresh whole egg. But if you want to eliminate a major source of dietary cholesterol, this replacement is a pretty good trade-off.

For a few months, whenever I mixed my egg replacement I added a drop of yellow food-coloring to make it *look* like a whole egg. Then it began to seem like a foolish make-believe and I stopped adding the color. Sometimes I add paprika, which gives me a pinkish egg. When I make an omelette with browned onion or cheese, the omelette gets some color that way.

Compared with a whole egg, the replacement doesn't have the binding quality that holds ingredients together so well in cookery. If I want a more adhesive product, as for croquettes or cheese ravioli, instead of one table-spoon of starch I use two tablespoons of raw Cream of Wheat and reduce the water to two ounces instead of three. I whirl the mixture in my blender, and it makes a substance about the consistency of sour cream.

Powdered egg white is used all the time in commercial baking and candy making and in ready-mixes, but it is seldom available at retail. Try coaxing a quarter of a pound from your bakery shop. If you do not succeed, and want to try using it, write me (c/o the publisher) and I'll tell you where you can get it by mail.

Let us say there are three kinds of foods—nutritive foods, fun foods, and junk foods. Of course, every food should be fun to eat, appetizing, "good for us" psychically as well as physically. But there are some foods we favor for their nutritional benefits, and that goes for most foods. We also find room in our diet for foods whose nutritional contribution is minimal but which add texture, color, or taste variety to our meals or snacks—mushrooms or grapes, for example. Junk foods are those that clutter up our diet and replace nutritious foods with products that are ready-made from refined food products, usually deriving their taste, color, and flavor from artificial ingredients, and offering relatively little food value. An example would be frozen waffles and syrup. Served with sausages, the meat provides the nutrients and makes the junk food a tolerable extravagance. But if you're doing without meat, you can't afford to crowd out the nutritious, natural food with junk food.

Does it take more time to eat vegetarian than to follow a conventional diet? You could start a lively discussion (or friendly argument) on this topic, and finally discover that it's a matter of taste—whether you like cold foods or hot, whether you start from scratch or use convenience foods, and so on. I think it takes a bit more time. I should expand that statement to say that for *me* it takes a bit more time to prepare the kind of food I like. But frankly I can't separate out the extra time I should ascribe to vegetarianism from the extra time I take for low-cholesterol cooking, and the extra time needed for cooking from scratch. As with many questions, the answer is so complicated, you might wish you hadn't asked. Some vegetarians insist they take *less* time to prepare meals than most conventional eaters. It takes *me* a little more time, but it's worth it.

I do most of my shopping at the supermarket, but I get some items (like sesame seeds, sunflower seeds, whole wheat flour) at a natural foods store, some items (like whole wheat graham crackers, Vita-Burger) at a health food store, and other items (like tofu, tapioca starch, dry soybeans, raw peanuts, bean sprouts, mock duck) at a Chinese grocery.

I try to limit the amount of time I spend shopping and cooking by buying nonperishables in larger quantities, and by preparing foods in larger quantities. The modern home freezer is truly a godsend. I make a dozen servings of soup at once, put them in six cartons of two servings each, label them, and stack them away in my freezer, ready to warm up and eat without any fuss or bother. It helps if I remember in the morning what I should defrost for the evening meal. It's silly to put a block of frozen food over the fire when, with a bit of forethought, you can let it defrost at room temperature during the day. When you come home it's ready to heat and eat.

One of my favorite make-ahead foods is a rice-and-soybean binder I developed, which I can use for making pancakes of all sorts. My strategy is to make the binder in larger quantities than I need, freeze it in servings for two, and then mix the binder with some fresh ingredient (like grated potatoes, cottage cheese, zucchini, or chopped spinach) just before frying. Here is my recipe for a batch that totals servings for eight (when mixed with vegetables or cottage cheese).

> 1 cup brown rice, uncooked
> ¼ cup dry soybeans, uncooked
> 4 egg replacements
> ½ cup water

Soak soybeans and rice in water overnight. (Add enough water over top of beans and rice to allow for expansion.) In a large bowl, mix drained rice, beans, eggs, and water. The standard home blender will handle about one-half of this mixture at a time. Run it through the blender at the highest speed. Each batch will take a few minutes to become a uniformly heavy cream, ready to pack in margarine tubs, label, and freeze.

The above recipe makes about three measuring cupfuls, which I divide into four margarine tubs. Each will make two or three servings mixed with about an equal quantity of grated potatoes or zucchini, chopped spinach, or cottage cheese.

If I'm making potato pancakes with my binder, I use two medium-size new potatoes, scrubbed clean but not peeled before grating. I add chopped green onions, vegetable bouillon granules, salt, pepper, paprika, and garlic powder. Often I fry just half the batter and let the other half stand in the refrigerator for a day. The potatoes darken a bit at the surface of the tub, but it tastes pretty good to me.

I have made pancakes with grated zucchini, a quantity about equal to the tub of binder. Season to taste. They will be less cohesive than the potato pancakes—be prepared to use two spatulas to turn them over. Fry them until they are brown on both sides. For spinach pancakes, I use a package of thawed (but not precooked) frozen chopped spinach, well-drained—I mean put the spinach in a sieve and push that excess water out! Season the spinach with oregano and dill (about one half-teaspoon each) to give the pancake a Greek spinach pie aroma. For cottage cheese pancakes, add a quantity about equal to the tub of binder, add parsley or green onion chopped, seasonings, and fry.

Note that my binder recipe uses rice and soybeans in the recommended proportions for protein complementarity.

Variety is the guiding principle for a healthy diet. Don't get stuck in a rut and live on little else but hard-boiled eggs, or canned tomato soup, or peanut butter on crackers. Each of the foregoing has its place in a diet that includes vegetables of all kinds—roots, stalks, and leaves (red, green, and yellow), fruits of all sorts, grains, seeds, and legumes, nuts, milk, and cheeses.

To have a varied and appetizing vegetarian menu, you don't have to adopt all sorts of exotic foods, but you may discover one or more new foods that you want to make part of your regular fare. I like yogurt, and make a two-week batch at a time. I don't care for tempeh, and can live without hummis or tabouli for long periods of time. Right now, tofu is an "in food" with natural food people, but it's what I would call a "fun food"—it's mainly water.[6] It has a jelly-like consistency and has little flavor of its own. Because it absorbs and extends flavor so well, it's a favorite in the Far East, where a few bits of meat or fish are cooked with a large quantity of vegetables. In vegetarian cooking, tofu is favored mainly for its interesting texture, a nice contrast when cubed and mixed with stir-fried vegetables. Sussman (in *The Vegetarian Alternative*) gives several tofu recipes.

To conclude this section with a nutritious sweet, I would like to offer a discovery of mine which I have named "Mary Jane," because it tastes like a favorite candy of my childhood. (These two-for-a-penny candies were made of molasses and peanut butter, and were wrapped in yellow wax paper.)

Blackstrap molasses is a very rich source of iron. To me, its taste is pleasant but powerful. I have found a simple and delicious way of using it, by mixing together three parts peanut butter to one part blackstrap molasses. At room temperature, they're easy to mix together. I keep the mixture refrigerated. Chilled, "Mary Jane" has the consistency of a moist brownie. I sometimes take a spoonful as a snack, or spread it on toast like peanut butter.

According to my calculations, "Mary Jane" is 67 percent richer in iron than plain peanut butter, and twice as rich in calcium.[7] A tablespoonful of "Mary Jane" has as much iron as two-thirds of a cup of steamed spinach. In both texture and taste, I like "Mary Jane" better than plain peanut butter, though I still use plain peanut butter for variety.

The topic of nutrition in its details is beyond the scope of this book. Preparing a vegetarian menu for a pregnant woman, an infant, or a growing child is a special responsibility. Vic Sussman takes these topics up in some detail in *The Vegetarian Alternative*. Nutritional information and recipes are contained in Lappé's *Diet for a Small Planet*, and in *Laurel's Kitchen*, by Robertson et al.

A word about eating out. Most restaurants have meatless specialties—cheese blintzes at a Jewish restaurant, spinach pie or Greek salad at a Greek restaurant (instead of pushing the anchovies aside, I ask the waiter to fix the salad with no anchovies and with extra feta cheese). Italian restaurants may serve cheese ravioli, eggplant parmigiana, spaghetti with meatless sauce, or pizza with everything but sausage. If I'm invited to dinner and meat is served, I play the "visiting anthropologist," and eat what is served. It's not my wish to make the hostess or other guests feel uncomfortable.[8] I would rather have declined the invitation than ask the hostess to cook me a separate meal. If the hostess knows my food preference, and serves up a vegetarian dinner for all, I feel especially honored.

Appendix II

Protein Complementarity

The proteins our bodies use are made up of twenty-two amino acid combinations. Eight of these amino acids can't be synthesized by our bodies; they must be obtained from outside sources. . . .

. . . Our bodies need each of the EAAs [essential amino acids] *simultaneously* in order to carry out protein synthesis. If one EAA is missing . . . protein synthesis will fall to a very low level or stop altogether.

And to complicate things further, we need the EAAs in different amounts. . . . Each EAA must be present in a given proportion.[1]

The simplest way to obtain the EAAs in the needed proportion is to eat those foods which already contain all eight EAAs in approximately the needed proportion. Milk, cheese, eggs, meat, fish, and poultry are such foods, and have therefore been glamourized by the term "complete protein foods." However, it is quite possible to "team up" foods that have complementary patterns of strengths and weaknesses, and eat them in a proportion that correctly approximates the proportion of EAAs required by the human body. This process of protein complementarity is illustrated graphically in Figure 1.

As Table 1 demonstrates, the nutritional advantage of eating complementary protein foods at the same meal and in specified proportions can be expressed as a *percentage gain* over eating the same foods separately. Combining the right protein foods in the right proportions is the heart of

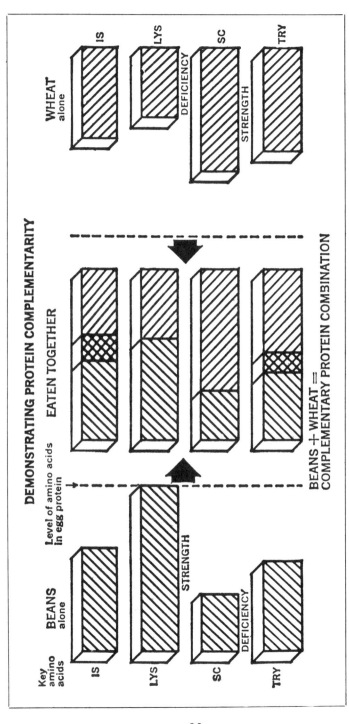

Fig. 1. Protein complementarity presented graphically. Reprinted from Lappé, *Diet for a Small Planet*, p. 82. Used by permission of the author. Source of Data: *Amino Acid Content of Foods and Biological Data on Proteins* (Rome: U.N. Food and Agricultural Organization, 1970).

Table 1

Protein Complementarity Presented Quantitatively

Example A. RICE AND BEANS (OR PEAS)

Eaten at the same meal, rice and beans yield 43 percent more usable protein than the same quantities of rice and beans eaten at separate meals. [Compare lines (4) and (5) below.]

Eaten at the same meal, rice and beans yield 97 percent more usable protein than the same total quantity of rice alone. [Compare lines (1) and (5) below.]

(1) 2 3/4 cups rice provides usable protein equivalent to 4.8 oz. steak.

(2) 2 cups rice provides usable protein equivalent to 3.5 oz. steak.

(3) 3/4 cup beans (or peas) provides usable protein equivalent to 3.1 oz. steak.

(4) If (2) and (3) are eaten at separate meals, they provide usable protein equivalent to 6.7 oz. steak.

(5) If (2) and (3) are eaten at the same meal, they provide usable protein equivalent to 9.5 oz. steak.

Example B. CORN MEAL AND BEANS (OR PEAS)

Eaten at the same meal, corn meal and beans yield 50 percent more usable protein than the same quantities of corn meal and beans eaten at separate meals. [Compare lines (4) and (5) below.]

Eaten at the same meal, corn meal and beans yield 170 percent more usable protein than the same total quantity of corn meal alone. [Compare lines (1) and (5) below.]

(1) 2 1/2 cups cornmeal provides usable protein equivalent to 1.8 oz. steak.

(2) 2 cups cornmeal provides usable protein equivalent to 1.5 oz. steak.

(3) 1/2 cup beans (or peas) provides usable protein equivalent to 2 oz. steak.

(4) If (2) and (3) are eaten at separate meals, they provide usable protein equivalent to 3.5 oz. steak.

(5) If (2) and (3) are eaten at the same meal, they provide usable protein equivalent to 5.25 oz. steak.

Adapted from Lappé, *Diet for a Small Planet*, pp. 362, 363.

Lappé's recommendations, contained throughout her pioneering book, *Diet for a Small Planet.*

More complicated to put into words and numbers than into routine culinary practice, protein combination is a feature of many traditional food combinations (listed on page 57). Before *any* protein—animal or vegetable—can be utilized by the body, it must be digested—each molecule "unstrung," so to speak, separated into its component amino acids. From this pool of amino acids, the human body assembles human proteins of various kinds, to grow and rebuild itself. Once a food combination is broken down (by enzyme action) into its constituent amino acids, the difference between "animal protein" and "vegetable protein" disappears. What is important is whether the body has the essential building blocks in the needed proportions.

"Minimal daily requirements" are probably of less concern to us than to scientists estimating how much protein food would be needed to prevent starvation in a population of a given size. We probably eat a little (or a lot) more than necessary, and how much is "enough" depends not only on age, sex, and weight, but on individual disposition. (If you'd like norms on daily protein requirements, you'll find them in the books by Vic Sussman and Frances Moore Lappé.)

Finally, I'd like to pass along a "rule of thumb" I go by, to assure that my meals (especially those which do not include egg or dairy products) have plenty of complete protein. From Table 1 you can see that a good ratio of grain to legume, for protein complementarity, is about four parts grain to one part legume. Therefore, I plan my main dish around some *grain* product:

bread (egg toast)	noodles
corn	rice
cornmeal	spaghetti (or other pasta)
macaroni	wheat bulgur (use it like rice)
matzos (fried)	

I then work in some legume as a secondary ingredient in my grain dish (e.g., green peas in my fried rice), or introduce a legume in a secondary dish (e.g., bean or lentil soup, side dish of green peas, a relish of cold kidney beans marinated in salad dressing), remembering to maintain an approximate ratio of four parts grain to one part legume.

Of course, there will be more to your meals than grain and legumes—salad vegetables, green vegetables, root vegetables, eggs, cheese, milk, fruits, nuts, seeds, and more. Variety is a key word in attaining a diet that is interesting, satisfying, and nutritionally balanced. Figure 2 summarizes what is known about complementary relationships not only between grain and legumes, but also between seeds and milk products, and between grain and milk products.

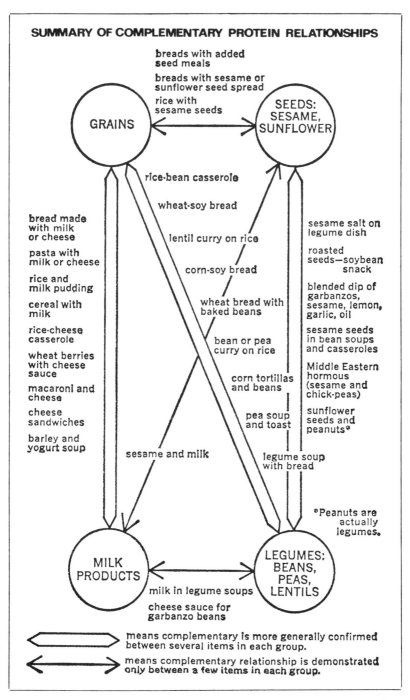

Fig. 2. Summary of complementary protein relationships. Reprinted from Lappé, *Diet for a Small Planet*, p. 153. Used with permission of the author.

Notes

Chapter 1

1. Genesis 1:29.
2. Frederick J. Simoons, *Eat Not This Flesh*, p. 25.
3. Ibid., p. 27.

Chapter 2

1. Deuteronomy 5:12-14.
2. Deuteronomy 22:10.
3. Deuteronomy 25:4.
4. *Shulchan Aruch*, vol. 4, chap. 186, p. 80.
5. Erich Isaac, "Forbidden Foods," p. 38.
6. Deuteronomy 22:4.
7. Deuteronomy 22:6.
8. Soncino Pentateuch, p. 843.
9. Proverbs 12:10.
10. Psalm 36:6-7.
11. Exodus 21:28.
12. Numbers 22:23-34.
13. Soncino Pentateuch, p. 673.
14. Ibid., p. 671.
15. *Shulchan Aruch*, vol. 2, p. 87.
16. Ibid., vol. 4, chap. 190, p. 84.
17. Isaac, p. 38.

18. Exodus 23:19, Deuteronomy 14:21. Maimonides conjectured that "meat boiled in milk . . . is . . . prohibited because it is somehow connected with idolatry, forming perhaps part of the service, or being used on some festival of the heathen" (*Guide for the Perplexed*, bk. 3, chap. 48). Rabbi Kook argued that the mixing of meat and milk is forbidden because it symbolizes both the moral wrong of denying a calf the natural enjoyment of its mother's breast and the "hard and cruel" practice of eating animal flesh (Kook, "Fragments," pp. 320-321).
19. Leviticus 22:28.
20. Soncino Pentateuch, p. 518.
21. Louis Jacobs, *What Does Judaism Say About* . . . ?, p. 182.
22. A rabbinical statement quoted to me by Mr. Philip L. Pick in a personal letter.
23. *Shulchan Aruch*, vol. 2, p. 29. The quotation is from Psalm 145:9.
24. Joe Green, *The Jewish Vegetarian Tradition*, p. 15.
25. Soncino Pentateuch, p. 843.
26. Ibid., p. 767. Rabbi Kook argues that these prohibitions serve in effect to *reprimand* man for animal mistreatment and slaughter ("Fragments," p. 319).

> The commandment to cover the blood of an animal or a bird captured while hunting focuses on the most apparent and conspicious inequity. These creatures are not fed by man, they impose no burden on him to raise them and develop them. [The commandment means] . . . Cover the blood! Hide your shame! These efforts will bear fruit, in the course of time people will be educated. . . . The regulation of slaughter . . . to reduce the pain of the animal registers a reminder that [animals] are not automatons devoid of life, but . . . living things. . . . The feelings of the animal, the sensitivity to its family attachment implied in the rule not to slaughter an ox or a sheep "with its young on the same day" . . . [and the injunction against taking birds from a nest while their mother looks on]—all these join in a mighty demonstration against the general inequity that stirs every heart.

27. Soncino Pentateuch, p. 854.
28. "We acknowledge that in a number of sects the slaughter of animals is forbidden out of a belief in the transmigration of souls; that is, it is believed that an animal may be inhabited by the soul of what once was a person. This belief is espoused by the Buddhists, Jainists, and by followers of Pythagoras. Transmigration of souls was also a belief of the later kabbalists, and this argument is used to justify vegetarianism in *Sedeh Hemed*, a monumental talmudic encyclopedia authored by Rabbi Hayyim Hezekia Medini (1837-1904)" (*Jewish Vegetarian*, Summer 1978, p. 35).
29. Harry Cohen, *A Basic Jewish Encyclopedia*, p. 75.
30. I Corinthians 9:9.
31. II Peter 2:12.
32. Erich Isaac points out that in Christian dogma, animals have been regarded as automata which *cannot* suffer, although they may give the deceptive appearance of suffering. It might be argued that Christianity needed a St. Francis of Assisi and an Albert Schweitzer to advocate kindness to animals, but Jewish law has always regarded animals as creatures which can suffer and must therefore be protected against needless suffering.

33. Genesis 1:29. The rabbis saw in this passage the clear implication that "the first man had not been allowed to eat meat" (*Sanhedrin* 59b, cited by Kook, "Fragments," p. 317).
34. Deuteronomy 8:7-9.
35. Louis Ginzberg, *Legends of the Bible*, p. 37.
36. Isaiah 11:6-7. Isaiah also prophesies that in the time of the Messiah work animals will be treated more appreciatively. Rabbi Kook renders Isaiah 30:24 as: "Oxen and asses that till the soil will eat their fodder savored with spices, winnowed with shovel and fan to remove the chaff."

Chapter 3

1. Simoons's study, *Eat Not This Flesh*, begins with an interest in food taboos. He becomes increasingly involved in man's treatment of animals as it becomes clear that food taboos usually relate to animal flesh rather than to other varieties of food.
2. Ibid., p. 126.
3. Ibid., p. 95.
4. Ibid., pp. 97, 98. See Simoons, p. 104, for reference to Langkavel.
5. In Peoria, Illinois, in 1959, a U.S. Army officer killed, skinned, and put a stray dog on a spit as a demonstration of military survival. He was prosecuted under an Illinois statute against cruelty to animals, pleaded guilty, and was fined $200 (Simoons, p. 91).
6. Ibid., pp. 53-54.
7. Ibid., p. 98.
8. Ibid., p. 97.
9. Ibid., p. 96.
10. Ibid., p. 58.
11. Ibid., p. 59.
12. Sally DeVore and Thelma White, *The Appetites of Man*, pp. 42-43.
13. Ibid., p. 42.
14. Simoons, p. 113.
15. Ibid., p. 36.
16. Ibid., p. 35.
17. Giehl, *Vegetarianism*, pp. 192-193.
18. Ibid., p. 192. In the same spirit, the present-day fishermen of the Japanese village of Katsumoto have erected a stone monument to honor the dolphins, which they stab to death by the thousands to protect their fishing industry. Each year villagers "gather at the dolphin monumnet to say prayers to Buddha and ask their victims for forgiveness. Some might call this hypocritical, but the people of Katsumoto say they do this out of respect" (*Chicago Tribune*, March 16, 1980).
19. Simoons, p. 33.
20. Ibid., p. 94.
21. Isaac, "Forbidden Foods," p. 39.
22. Reay Tannahill, *Food in History*, p. 103.
23. Vic Sussman, *The Vegetarian Alternative*, pp. 179-180.

24. Simoons, p. 11.
25. Ibid.
26. Ibid., p. 12.
27. Isaac makes the observation that the ban against carcasses of animals that appear to have been mutilated served notice to their owners to take the best care of their animals or suffer an economic penalty, as an animal declared *trefe* had little economic worth (p. 39). The *shochet* may become an expert at detecting *visible* signs of pathology, but in today's world the health of the consumer is endangered by contaminants which, though invisible, pose serious health hazards. Insecticide residues which accidentally end up in animal tissue, hormonal food supplements and antibiotics which are deliberately introduced into the animal's system to accelerate growth and prevent disease— these are risks that the Talmudic rabbis did not dream of. The existence of these invisible contaminants raises the question: Can animal flesh as it is produced today be pronounced *kasher* in the original spirit of the word?
28. A pioneer insight into "the meaning of infancy" is contained in Fiske's essay by that title. For a modern anthropologist's treatment of the subject, see LaBarre, *The Human Animal.*
29. Freud, *Civilization and Its Discontents*, pp. 139-140.
30. Bohannon, p. 136.
31. Deidentification is the label applied by van den Haag to the psychological mechanism that may redefine a person as "perfectly natural to kill." A volunteer on the Republican side in the Spanish Civil War in 1938, Simone Weil observed how Republican soldiers were able to regard the Nationalists not as countrymen but as combat enemies. Wrote Miss Weil, "I felt that whenever a certain group of human beings is relegated, by some temporal or spiritual authority, beyond the pale of those whose life has a price, then one finds it perfectly natural to kill such people. When one knows one can kill without risk or punishment or blame, one kills . . . " (van den Haag, pp. 126-127).

Chapter 4

1. Genesis 9:2-4.
2. Genesis 6:11.
3. This permission is given in Deuteronomy 12:15 and repeated in 12:20: "Thou mayest kill and eat flesh . . . after all the desire of they soul." The standard translations may be misleadingly poetic. Rabbi Kook renders this passage as "Because you lust after eating meat—then you may slaughter and eat." Rabbi Kook comments that "there is indeed a hidden reprimand between the lines of Torah" in that sanction ("Fragments," p. 318).
4. Jean Soler, "The Dietary Prohibitions of the Hebrews." Soler asks: "Has there been an attempt, historically, to impose a vegetarian regime on the Hebrews? . . . The Bible does contain traces of such an attempt or, at any rate, of such an ideal" (p. 25).
5. Numbers 11:7.
6. Soler, p. 25.
7. Numbers 11:19-20.

8. Soler, p. 25.
9. Job 15:16.
10. Kook, "Vision."
11. In "Fragments," Rabbi Kook writes: "When the animal lust for meat became over-powering, if the flesh of all living things had been forbidden, then the moral destruc-tiveness, which will always appear at such times, would not have differentiated between man and animal. . . . The knife, the axe, the guillotine, the electric current, would have felled them all alike in order to satisfy the vulgar craving of . . . humanity" (pp. 318-319).
12. Kook "Vision." In "Fragments," Rabbi Kook prophesies: "The hidden yearning to act justly toward animals [will] emerge at the proper time" (p. 318).
13. R. D. Jameson (in his article "Cannibalism") mentions the myths of Odysseus and the Cyclops and of Tantalus and Pelops as having a cannibal motif.
14. Jameson refers to *Hansel and Gretel* and *Jack the Giant-Killer*. In many European variants of these folktales, "a parent either eats the children or threatens to. Other tales are about a parent who sent the child to be killed, but must have the heart or liver returned, or about the mother who sent a child prepared as a stew to its father, or about husbands and wives who trick each other into eating their lovers similarly disguised" (ibid., p. 189).
15. Tannahill asserts that in prehistoric times, cannibalism was not reserved for magical practices or times of famine, but was a routine dietary practice. "The domestic debris of Peking man's caves consists mainly of broken-up bones of animals he hunted for food, but there are also a number of human bones, fractured in much the same way, some of them split to give access to . . . the marrow. This implies not only that he was prepared to eat his fellows when the hunting was poor, but that he ate them [along with] deer,otter, [and] wild sheep" (*Flesh and Blood*, p. 3).
16. "During the anarchic conditions of the eleventh century, human meat became a commonplace" in northern China. Tannahill describes human-meat restaurants of that time (ibid., p. 46).
17. When the Spaniards discovered the New World, they observed cannibalism of a highly developed sort among the Aztecs, whose religion, military practices, and domestic economy were all directed toward obtaining a regular supply of human flesh. For details of this way of life, see Tannahill, *Flesh and Blood*, pp. 84-85.
18. Tannahill recounts many instances, from various periods and different parts of the world, of people turning to cannibalism during times of famine. For example: "In A.D. 450 there was a famine in Italy when parents ate their children. Between 695 and 700 England and Ireland suffered from a three-year dearth during which 'men ate each other.' It was the turn of Bulgaria and Germany to starve in 845 and 851, and in 936 began a four-year famine in Scotland when 'people began to devour one another.' In the latter half of the tenth century . . . 'a mighty famine' swept the whole Romanised world for five years. . . . So severe was the famine that young men ate their mothers and, forgetting all maternal instincts, mothers ate their little ones" (Tannahill, *Flesh and Blood*, pp. 46-47).
19. Ibid., p. 143.
20. *Khrushchev Remembers*.

21. *Flesh and Blood*, pp. 174-175.
22. Simoons, *Eat Not This Flesh*, pp. 8-9.
23. Hogg, "Cannibalism and Human Sacrifice."
24. Isaiah 11:7.

Chapter 5

1. Behrman House, 1962.
2. Soncino Pentateuch, p. 201.
3. Ibid., pp. 558-559.
4. Ibid., p. 401. In "Fragments," Rabbi Kook likewise argues that the mode of Temple worship was intended to express "the broadest and most spiritual ideals" in a language so simple "that even a child can understand." Animal sacrifice is described as a medium that linked "the lofty and the lowly" (p. 316).
5. Thus, says Rabbi Hertz, "The *manner* of worship in use among the peoples of antiquity was retained, but that worship was now directed towards the One and Holy God." Through the redefinition of animal sacrifice, wrote Maimonides, "idolatry was eradicated, and the vital principle of our Faith, the existence and unity of God, was firmly established—without confusing the minds of the people by the abolition of sacrificial worship, to which they were accustomed" (Soncino Pentateuch, p. 486). Robert Alter ("A New Theory of Kashrut," p. 50) credits the Israeli Bible scholar Yehezkel Kaufmann with developing this theme.
6. Leviticus 20:2. In Psalm 106 human sacrifice is mentioned as one of the sins of past generations—the worship of the golden calf, the worship of Baal, and the offering of "the blood of sons and daughters . . . to the gods of Canaan" (Psalm 106:38).
7. Soler, p. 26.
8. Soncino Pentateuch, p. 413.
9. The attainment of holiness may sound like a strange goal to a modern secular reader, but as we continue to read Leviticus, we see holiness "operationally defined" as finding a heterosexual partner outside the family, practicing generosity to the less fortunate, and dealing fairly with the stranger. "Holiness" turns out to be not so different from "psychological maturity," or becoming a real person, a *mensch*.
10. Stefansson, in *Not by Bread Alone*, points out that animal fat, in some cultures, is a highly prized portion of the animal carcass. This was the part that was sacrificed in a Temple offering. Stefansson points to the positive references to *fat* in the Hebrew Bible—"You shall eat the fat of the land" (Genesis 45:18). Rabbi Kook also regards the eating of fat (and the drinking of blood) as the indulgence of a "vulgar craving." By prohibiting fat and blood, it is as if God says: "If, by necessity, to strengthen your prowess, you slaughter the animal . . . you raised by your own exertion, do not indulge in this to satisfy the vulgar craving that lusts for fat." Rabbi Kook adds: "When the savage luxury of eating fat and blood . . . is forbidden, it takes away the worst element of this cruel gluttony" ("Fragments," p. 320).

11. Milgrom, "Leviticus," cols. 139-140, 142.
12. Leviticus 19:34.
13. Leviticus 24:22.
14. Leviticus 19:18. "Hillel paraphrased this rule into 'Whatever is hateful unto thee do it not to thy fellow'; and declared it to be the whole Law, the remainder being but a commentary on this fundamental principle of the Torah" (Soncino Pentateuch, p. 502).
15. A basis for this misconception are the words that Jesus is said to have directed to his disciples: "*A new commandment I give unto you*, That ye love one another; as I have loved you, that ye also love one another" (John 13:34, emphasis added). In an earlier chapter of the New Testament, a Pharisee challenges Jesus to recite the most important commandment of the tradition. Jesus' answer includes the words: "Thou shalt love thy neighbor as thyself" (Mark 12:31). The scribe agrees: " . . . to love his neighbor as himself, is more than all whole burnt offerings and sacrifices" (Mark 12:33).

   Judaism taught unselfishness before Christianity did, simply because Judaism is older than Christianity. All major religions of the world, writes anthropologist P. Bohannan, hold as their most basic tenet that "unselfishness is the primary virtue and that selfishness lies at the root of the world's ills" (*Social Anthropology*, p. 336).
16. Soncino Pentateuch, pp. 497-498.
17. Birnbaum reconstructs the feasting and banqueting that accompanied Temple offerings: "When the festal season came around . . . multitudes of people streamed into the Temple from all directions, marching joyfully to the sound of music, and bearing with them bread and wine to set forth the feast, which meant open-handed hospitality. . . . portions were distributed freely to rich and poor" (*A Book of Jewish Concepts*, p. 550). Birnbaum's reconstruction may be based in part on the prophet Isaiah's lamentation that in a time of crisis, instead of prayer he saw "joy and merry-making, slaughtering of cattle and killing of sheep, eating of meat and drinking of wine, as you thought, Let us eat and drink; for tomorrow we die" (Isaiah 22:13).
18. Isaiah 1:11.
19. Hosea 6:6.
20. Psalm 50:1, 8-13.
21. Jeremiah 7:9, 21, 30.
22. We should distinguish between the excesses of Temple sacrifice, which were abhorrent to Christians and Hebrew prophets alike, and the *concept* of a blood sacrifice, which became central to Christian doctrine. Christ is heralded with the words, "Behold the Lamb of God, which taketh away the sin of the world" (John 1:29). In John 6:56, Jesus is quoted to say, "He that eateth my flesh, and drinketh my blood, dwelleth in me, and I in him." The Christian scholar Erdman describes Christ as "the perfect sacrifice" (*The Book of Leviticus*, p. 25), and interprets the entire Book of Leviticus as a prophecy of the coming of "the perfect Sacrifice."
23. Harris, *A Thousand Years of Jewish History*, p. 188.
24. Ibid.

Chapter 6

1. The incongruity between the sanction of animal slaughter and worship of a God who has mercy on all that lives is at the forefront of Rabbi Jacob Cohen's *The Royal Table*, an outline of the Jewish dietary laws. The opening sentence of his book is: "In the perfect world originally designed by God, man was meant to be a vegetarian." On the same page begins a quotation from *Sifre*, "Insomuch as all animals possess a certain degree of intelligence and consciousness, it is a waste of this divine gift, and an irreparable damage to destroy them" (pp. 9-10).
2. Baba Batra 60b.
3. Pesahim 109a.
4. Bruce, "Asceticism," col. 678.
5. Quoted by Isaiah Berman, *Shehita*, p. 33.
6. Baba Batra 60b.
7. The phrase is Berman's, ibid., p. 32.
8. Harry A. Cohen, *A Basic Jewish Encyclopedia*, p. 125.
9. Berman, p. 13.
10. Freedman, *The Book of Kashruth*, pp. 30-31.
11. Maimonides, *Mishneh Torah*, p. 134.
12. Ibid, p. 135 fn.
13. Berman, p. 8.
14. Ibid., pp. 138-139.
15. Freedman, p. 106.
16. Berman, p. 1.
17. Berman offers the following illustrative note: "The Jewish peddlers, who in the 1830s hawked their wares through an English countryside devoid of Jewish homes and hotels, would supply themselves with kosher meat for their Sabbath meals by organizing themselves into Sabbath clubs. Each club would arrange to spend its Sabbath at a designated . . . inn. Early Friday morning . . . one of its members would arrive at the place and prepare the meals for the entire group" (p. 2). The same author quotes a non-Jewish observer of the turn of the century: "The most important thing for the Catholic or the Protestant when he is traveling is to find a church, a chapel, a priest to say mass, or a clergyman to preach a sermon. In the eyes of the most devout Jew the synagogue is a secondary consideration; the vital thing is the butcher shop and the *shohet*" (quoted from *Israel Among the Nations*, by Anatole Leroy-Bealieu, translated by Frances Hellman [New York, 1895], p. 133).
18. Berman (in his Acknowledgments) recalls that when he was serving as rabbi in Rochester, New York, in the 1930s, slaughtering fees were collected by a Jewish community board. These fees not only paid for the *shochet* and meat-shop inspectors, but also supported the community's Hebrew school, ritual bath, and some Orthodox rabbis. New York City, he recalls, had no such system.
19. Still hoping to cope with a trying situation, the *Israelitisches Familienblatt* for 1933 offered four articles on how to prepare simple meatless meals—"Kuchenzettel fur die einfache fleishlose Kuche" (Berman, pp. 260-261).

20. Freedman, p. 123.
21. Ibid., p. 124.
22. Ibid., pp. 125-126.
23. Ibid., p. 130.
24. Ibid., p. 95.
25. Ibid., p. 100.
26. Ibid., p. 103.
27. Rabinowitz, "Rabbinics v. Vegetarianism," p. 34.
28. Ibid.
29. Ibid.
30. Freedman, p. 86.
31. Sol Friedman, "Kashruth and Civil Kosher Law Enforcement," p. 78.
32. Ibid. p. 78.
33. Israel Shenker, *Noshing is Sacred*, p. 61.
34. Ibid., p. 58.
35. Freedman, p. 93.
36. Shenker, pp. 41-43.
37. Ibid., p. 53.
38. Ibid., p. 47.
39. Freedman, p. 74.
40. In Levin and Boyden's *Kosher Code* appear the words: "It is the custom of the heathen . . . to spay the rooster, in order to make them fat, and to sew up the place of incision. It is customary [for Jews] to eat these roosters, because those who spay them are competent to perform this feat without touching the intestines" (p. 136 fn.).
41. Maimonides, *Guide for the Perplexed*, pt. 3, chap. 48, p. 253.
42. Liebman cites studies conducted in Washington, D.C., Philadelphia, and Providence (p. 34).
43. The observation is offered by Polner, *Rabbi: The American Experience*, pp. 20 and 51.
44. Isaac, p. 51. Commenting on the declining popularity of the dietary laws, Rabbi Stuart Rosenberg notes that during the 1960s this indifference was "flouted officially by the organized Jewish community itself. Dinners sponsored by the comprehensive communal charity, the Welfare Fund and Federation, were often no longer served in accordance with the dietary laws. And after World War II, a number of Jewish hospitals built with capital funds collected from all sections of the Jewish community, the Orthodox included, openly refused to run kosher kitchens for their patients, on the grounds that their institutions were 'non-sectarian.' (Insistent Jewish patients would, of course, be offered kosher food, but only 'on request.')

"Increasingly, the few kosher restaurants that had always been found in the larger metropolitan areas were forced to close because of a growing scarcity of customers," Rabbi Rosenberg continues. "Fewer and fewer Jews were '100 percent kosher': more and more of those who may have retained some semblance of the religious dietary practices in their own homes . . . consistently disregarded them in public. . . . The 'non-observant Orthodox Jew,' that uniquely American phenomenon, was everywhere in sight" (Rosenberg, pp. 226-228).

45. In a 1957 issue of *Conservative Judaism*, Rabbi Hershel Matt wrote, "The Conservative movement has not articulated how it stands on kashrut and its own adherents are uncomfortable, embarrassed, and confused" (pp. 34-35). In the same issue, the editor of the journal wrote, "I have no statistics to draw from, but I would not hesitate to estimate that of American Jewish homes today [1957!] where husband and wife are forty years of age or less, relatively few are kosher" (Dresner, pp. 1-2).

46. It could be argued that one of the unwanted effects of the *kashrut* laws today is that they *divide* the Jewish people into those who "keep kosher" and those who do not, and maintain a social barrier between these two camps. Does this barrier enrich or impoverish Jewish life? An observant Jew, for example, does not want his child to marry a person whose *parents* do not keep kosher (although the prospective mate has adopted traditional Jewish rituals), since observant parents cannot socialize freely with nonobservant in-laws!

Perhaps the need in our times is not so much for ways to keep Jews separate from other peoples as for strategies that bring Jews together. And vegetarianism is one way that Jews can be brought together to rediscover their common heritage.

Chapter 7

1. Jerusalem Talmud, Nedarim 9:1.
2. Kiddushin, at the end.
3. Midrash on Lamentations 3.
4. Erubin 54a.
5. Taanit 11a.
6. Hullin 84a.
7. Andre Neher and Yaacov Mazor, "Hasidism," col. 1405.
8. *Webster's New World Dictionary*, 1957.
9. Deuteronomy 7:15.
10. Exodus 15:26.
11. *Guide for the Perplexed*, pt. III.
12. Ibid., pt. III, chap. 46.
13. *Akedath Yitzchak*, Lev. XI, Gate 60; quoted from Friedman, p. 48.
14. "Fragments," p. 321.
15. Friedman, pp. 42-43.
16. Deuteronomy 4:40.
17. Proverbs 3:16-18.
18. Leviticus 18:5.
19. Leo Levi, in *Vistas from Mount Moriah*, notes that more than 2,000 Biblical and Talmudic quotations related to health are brought together in *Biblisch-Talmudische Medizin* by Julius Preuss (Berlin: Karger, 1923; reprint, New York: Ktav, 1971). This classic work is also available in an English translation by Fred Rosner (New York: Sanhedrin Press, 1978).
20. Arturo Castiglioni, "The Contribution of the Jews to Medicine," p. 1353.

21. Shabbat 108b.
22. Sotah 4b.
23. Julius Greenstone, "Health Laws."
24. Nedarim 81a.
25. Greenstone, "Health Laws."
26. Baba Kamma 60b.
27. Hullin 10a.
28. Pesachim 114a.
29. Midrash on Exodus 14.
30. Nedarim 8b.
31. Baba Bathra 60b, Shabbat 18a, Betzah 22b.
32. Yalkut Shimoni 184.
33. Baba Metzia 26a.
34. Sanhedrin 17a.
35. Erubin 21a.
36. Avodah Zarah 12b.
37. Jerusalem Talmud, Terumot 8:5.
38. Jacob Levy, "Hygiene, Jewish."
39. Tosefta, Baba Bathra 1.
40. Kethubot 110b.
41. Greenstone, "Health Laws."
42. Berachot 62b.
43. Gittin 70a.
44. Ibid.
45. Shabbat 9b.
46. Taanit 5a.
47. Pesachim 11a, Baba Metzia 107b.
48. Ibid.
49. Yoma 75b.
50. Yoma 74b.
51. Greenstone, "Health Laws."
52. Shabbat 152a.
53. Shabbat 41a.
54. Berachot 44a.
55. Tosefta, Berachot 4.
56. Mechilta, Beshalla.
57. Pesikta Rabbathi, Ekeb.
58. Midrash Ruth 3.
59. Berachot 40a.
60. Gittin 70a, Sukkah 49b, Baba Bathra 58a, Shabbat 20a.
61. Hullin 84a.
62. Shabbat 140b, Baba Kamma 82a, Shabbat 108a, Berachot 51a, 44b, 94a.
63. Shabbat 83a, Kethubot 10b, Zohar 3:40.
64. Menachot 85b.

65. Levy, "Hygiene, Jewish."
66. Yoma 75a.
67. Sifre, Korah 119.
68. Hirsch Loeb Gordon, "Hygiene of the Jews."
69. Shabbat 151b.
70. Levy, "Hygiene, Jewish."
71. Nedarim 49b.
72. Greenstone, "Health Laws."
73. Aboth de Rabbi Nathan 9.
74. Hullin 24b.
75. Jerusalem Talmud, Terumot 8:2.
76. Jerusalem Talmud, Shabbat 14.
77. Tanna Debe Eliyahu 3.
78. Pesachim 25a.
79. Shabbat 132a.
80. Tosefta, Shabbat 16.
81. Hullin 10a.
82. Ibid.
83. Castiglioni, p. 1353.
84. Ecclesiastes 7:12.
85. Jerusalem Talmud, Taanit 6:3.
86. Proverbs 3:1, 13, 16, 18.
87. Berachot 60a.
88. Levi, p. 62.
89. Ibid., Preface.

Chapter 8

1. The anthropological information contained in this chapter is largely taken from Howell, *Early Man*, an excellent introduction to paleoanthropology recommended by my colleague Professor Charles Warren.
2. The conjecture that early man was a scavenger is based on the high proportion of skull and leg bones found in caves where early men are believed to have lived. Carnivores do not ordinarily drag bones to their lairs. Typically, they eat the soft parts and leave the rest in the open field (Howell, pp. 64-65). An echo of man's scavenger past is contained in the Biblical commandment that forbids eating the flesh of an animal that has been killed by a wild beast (Exodus 22:30).
3. "While the women gather nuts, the men hunt . . . " (Howell, p. 183). This observation of life among present-day Bushmen is suggestive of the division of labor that prevailed between men and women in a hunting society. Pregnancy, nursing, and child care were likely to keep women at home while the men went hunting. Food-gathering and preparation were other tasks which women could perform close by the camp or cave. If the hunters returned exhausted but empty-handed, the women's

gatherings would be more than welcome. Undoubtedly, a hunting economy sharpened the differences between the sex roles, compared with an economy of plant-food gathering.

4. Tannahill suggests that roasting and grinding began as attempts to separate the chaff from the grain, a difficult task with wild varieties of grain (*Food in History*, pp. 33-38, 68).

5. Simoons, *Eat Not This Flesh*, pp. 7-8.

6. DeVore and White, *The Appetites of Man*, p. 66.

7. See ibid., p. 53, for a recipe for *imjudara*, Tuareg lentil and wheat stew.

8. See ibid., p. 78, for a recipe for Hunza barley and garbanzo curry.

9. Both Sussman (*The Vegetarian Alternative*, p. 83) and Mayer (*Human Nutrition*) acknowledge W. C. Rose's unique contribution to modern knowledge of human nutritional needs—the identification of the essential amino acids. Writes Mayer: "It is . . . to Rose that we are indebted for a clear and detailed knowledge of indispensable amino acids" (1972, p. 78).

10. Older writings may overemphasize the need to ingest all the essential amino acids in the ideal balance in order to obtain the needed amount of needed protein. In the early 1970s several studies were published showing that there is always present in the gut and bloodstream "a constant pool of amino acids . . . coming from the continual breakdown of intestinal wall cells, tissue proteins, and digestive secretions. When *food* amino acids are ingested, they mix with this reserve of internal amino acids. The process thus acts to even out any temporary . . . imbalance, such as might occur in a single meal" (Sussman, p. 87). The body recycles scarce materials!

11. "Learn from all men" is, of course, an ambiguous statement. It can mean, "Learn from every individual person," or "Learn from what *all men* hold to be true. Be guided by the consensus." Both meanings of the words are worth observing. A scientific vegetarianism would give every viewpoint a hearing and at the same time respect the consensus of the scientific community. I would reserve my sharpest disagreement for those who disregard the principles of the scientific community in favor of a chosen *philosophical* guide to nutrition.

Chapter 9

1. *Jewish Vegetarian*, Autumn 1974, p. 27. Rabbi Maccoby was all but forgotten by the present generation until the Jewish Vegetarian Society learned and documented what was known about this pioneer Jewish vegetarian. A portrait of Rabbi Maccoby now occupies a place of honor in the London headquarters of the Jewish Vegetarian Society.

2. Ibid., September 1966, p. 29.

3. Joseph Leftwich, in *Tree of Life*, p. 8.

4. "A Vegetarian Cookbook in Yiddish," in Pick, *Tree of Life*, pp. 94-95.

5. *Jewish Vegetarian*, November 1977, pp. 29-30.

6. Groner, "The Greening of Kashrut," p. 12.

7. *Jewish Vegetarian*, August 1973, p. 42.
8. Agnon, *The Bridal Canopy*, pp. 222-223.
9. Singer, *The Manor*, p. 349.
10. *Jewish Vegetarian*, November 1977, p. 30.

Chapter 10

1. Louis Jacobs, *What Does Judaism Say About . . . ?*
2. Maimonides, *Mishneh Torah*, p. 11.
3. Williams, *Nutrition in a Nutshell*, p. 43.
4. Williams, *Biochemical Individuality*.
5. Groner, "The Greening of Kashrut," p. 16.
6. Ibid., p. 20.
7. Ibid.
8. Robertson et al., *Laurel's Kitchen*, p. 39.
9. Kook, "Vision."
10. The thought expresses the Jewish tradition, but the words are those of John Dewey, in *A Common Faith*.
11. Agus, *Abraham Isaac Kook*, p. xii.
12. Koppel and Kaufman, "Elie Wiesel," p. 13.
13. In the February 1979 issue of *Commentary*, Ruth R. Wisse translates this paragraph from a 1974 Yiddish novel of Singer's, *Der Baal Tschuva (The Penitent)*, characterizing this work as "a novel intended for Yiddish readers, that is not likely to succeed in English." The author of the article claims that the character in the novel to whom the quotation is ascribed, "despite a technical separation from the author [Singer] clearly speaks with his full blessing" (p. 38).
14. The psychoanalyst who wrote most extensively on Jewish ritual is Theodor Reik. So far as I have been able to discover, he had nothing to say about *kashrut*. His favorite ritual for discussion was, of course, circumcision, and there are no less than twenty-three references to this rite in *Dogma and Compulsion*. The index of that book mentions Bar Mitzvah, Day of Atonement, *kaddish*, mezuzah, mourning customs, *niddah*, phylacteries, prayer shawl, ritual cleanliness, Sabbath, *sukkah*, *zizzith*—but nothing on dietary laws, *kashrut*, or food avoidances! In Reik's *Mystery on the Mountain*, the index lists several references for Bar Mitzvah, Passover, sacrifices, Sabbath, and circumcision—but nothing is said about dietary laws!
15. Grollman writes that a friend once expressed to Freud misgivings about bringing up his infant son as a Jew, growing up in anti-Semitic Austria. Advised Freud: "If you do not let your son grow up as a Jew, you will deprive him of those sources of energy which cannot be replaced by anything else. He will have to struggle as a Jew and you ought to develop in him all the energy he will need for that struggle. Do not deprive him of that advantage" (pp. 83-84). Elsewhere Grollman notes that of Freud's six children, "none ever became converted or entered into a mixed marriage" (p. 78).

16. In Freud's own words, "Devout believers are safeguarded in a high degree against the risk of certain neurotic illnesses; their acceptance of the universal neurosis spares them the task of constructing a personal one" (*Future of an Illusion*, p. 72).
17. Ibid., p. 34.
18. Rubenstein, "The Making of a Rabbi," p. 263.
19. Is it proper for a religious adherent to be kept in chronic doubt about the performance of a ritual that he is, in principle, quite familiar with? One gets the impression that questions about "keeping kosher" continue to burden, or at least actively concern, traditional Jews. In Chicago, a group of rabbinical students maintain a Jewish information "hot line," through which they offer to find answers to questions about *anything* related to Jewish life. In 1978 a *majority* of their telephone calls concerned questions of *kashrut!*

    Silberman writes in the *Encyclopaedia Britannica* that the original effect of the Jewish home rituals was to democratize religious practice, by shifting the emphasis from special-occasion ceremonies performed by Temple priests to everyday rituals performed by ordinary persons in their own homes. Over the centuries, Silberman admits, the spirit of hallowing the everyday became transformed, and he suggests that halachic rules may serve defensive purposes.

    One is reminded of the Talmudic rejection of perpetual meat-abstention—"Regulations that are too onerous for the community to bear should not be imposed" (Baba Bathra 60b) and wonders whether this guideline applies to the traditional *kashrut* today.
20. Buber, *Hasidism and Modern Man*, pp. 32-33.

Appendix I

1. See Lappé, *Diet for a Small Planet*, pp. 278-280, for tables on comparisons between whole wheat and white flour, brown and white rice, sugars, honey, and molasses. For example, the following figures compare granulated sugar, honey, and blackstrap molasses.

	Granulated White Sugar	Strained Honey	Blackstrap Molasses
*Minerals**			
calcium	0	5	684
phosphorous	0	6	84
iron	0.1	0.5	16.1
sodium	1.0	5	96
potassium	3.0	51	2927

Vitamins *

thiamine	0	trace	0.11
riboflavin	0	0.04	0.19
niacin	0	0.3	2.0

*mg per 100 g or 3½ oz.

Few differences between similar foods are as dramatic as these, but the perusal of food-value tables can sometimes be a rewarding experience.

2. There have been dramatic health claims made for lecithin. This substance is a significant part of the egg yolk, and occurs naturally in human and animal tissue. Quite aside from its claimed health value, lecithin is widely used in the candy and paint (!) industries for its properties as a homogenizer of oily and aqueous substances. It is for the emulsifying, or *blending*, property of lecithin that I find it so useful—so far as I am concerned, its nutritional contribution is a "bonus."

   For those who are worried about using "additives" in their cookery, it should be added that liquid lecithin is a by-product from pressing oil from soybeans. Lecithin is drawn off when the oil is purified. In its natural state, lecithin is a heavy liquid. It may be converted to granules, I suppose, for ease of handling, measuring, and packaging. I prefer the natural liquid product.

3. Stefansson, chap. 6.

4. If you're asking how to know whether to use okra or gumbo filé, why not use a combination of both. In your next stew or soup, try a handful of cut okra and one or two teaspoonfuls of filé.

5. Groner, "The Greening of Kashrut," p. 13.

6. The following table compares cooked peas, cooked soybeans, and tofu.

	Calories	Protein	Carbo-hydrate	Fiber	Vitamin A	Potassium	Calcium
		g	g	g	(IU)	mg	mg
cooked soybeans, 1 cup	234	20	19	2.9	50	970	130
tofu, piece 2½x2¼x1-inch	86	9.4	3	.1	0	50	150
cooked peas, 1 cup	338	24	60	4.9	120	1000	64

Source: Food table in Robertson et al., *Laurel's Kitchen*, pp. 548-549.

   It is hard to find a nutritional basis for the considerable popularity of tofu among natural food users and among vegetarians. This should alert the reader to the existence of fads and fashions in natural foods, as in other domains of human affairs.

7. The following figures compare the mineral-value of peanut butter, blackstrap molasses, and a mixture of 75 percent peanut butter and 25 percent blackstrap molasses, which I have dubbed "Mary Jane."

	Peanut Butter**	Blackstrap Molasses**	75% Peanut Butter 25% Blackstrap**
*Minerals**			
calcium	25.8	157	49
phosphorous	17.1	17	17
iron	.87	3.2	1.45
sodium	273	19	208.75
potassium	282	585	375.25

*mg
**1 tablespoonful or 20 grams

8. Comments a vegetarian rabbinical student: "It always seems like an insult to my hosts when I refuse to eat meat at the *Shabbat* table" (Groner, p. 20). In the Talmud appears the sentence, "There is no happiness without meat." Writes Groner: "The association of meat with *simcha* is so strong, that it has prompted some *halachic* vegetarians to eat a symbolic piece of chicken on festive occasions" (p. 14). To share the spirit of a *simcha*, to avoid dampening someone's *simcha* (*fershtechen a simcha*) are important values in Jewish life, and deserve priority over absolute consistency in vegetarian practice.

Appendix II

1. Lappé, *Diet for a Small Planet*, p. 36. For a more complete discussion of protein biochemistry, see Lappé, pp. 34-40, or Sussman, *The Vegetarian Alternative*, pp. 80-88. A basic presentation of protein biochemistry is contained in chapter 3 of Williams, *Nutrition in a Nutshell*, pp. 23-36.

Bibliography

Agnon, S. Y. *The Bridal Canopy*. New York: Schocken Books, 1976.

Agus, Jacob. Preface I to *Abraham Isaac Kook*, edited and translated by Ben Zion Bokser. New York: Paulist Press, 1978.

Alter, Robert. "A New Theory of Kashrut." *Commentary*, August 1979, pp. 46-52.

"A Vegetarian Cookbook in Yiddish." In *Tree of Life*, edited by Philip L. Pick. New York: A. S. Barnes, 1977.

Berman, Isaiah. *Shehita: A Study in the Cultural and Social Life of the Jewish People*. New York: Bloch, 1941.

Birnbaum, Philip. *A Book of Jewish Concepts*. New York: Hebrew Publishing Co., 1964.

Bohannan, P. *Social Anthropology*. New York: Holt, Rinehart & Winston, 1963.

Bruce, Frederick Fyvie. "Asceticism." *Encyclopaedia Judaica* (1972), vol. 2, cols. 680-682.

Buber, Martin. *Hasidism and Modern Man*. New York: Horizon Press, 1958.

Caro, Joseph. *Shulchan Aruch* [Code of Jewish Law]. Venice, 1564. References in this volume are taken from the translation by Hyman E. Goldin. New York: Hebrew Publishing Co., 1927. Pages in this edition are numbered as if it were printed in four volumes.

Castiglioni, Arturo. "The Contribution of the Jews to Medicine." In *The Jews: Their History, Culture and Religion*, edited by Louis Finkelstein. 3d edition. Philadelphia: Jewish Publication Society, 1960.

Cohen, Harry A. *A Basic Jewish Encyclopedia*. Hartford, Conn.: Hartmore House, 1965.

Cohen, Jacob. *The Royal Table: An Outline of the Dietary Laws of Israel*. 1936. Reprint. Jerusalem: Philipp Feldheim, 1970.

DeVore, Sally, and Thelma White. *The Appetites of Man*. Garden City, N.Y.: Doubleday Anchor Books, 1978. (Originally published as *Dinner's Ready*, 1977.)

Dewey, John. *A Common Faith*. New Haven, Conn.: Yale University Press, 1934.

Dresner, Samuel H. "The Mitzvah of Kashrut: The Meaning of the Dietary Laws for Our Time." *Conservative Judaism*, Fall 1957, pp. 1-15.

Erdman, Charles. *The Book of Leviticus*. New York: Fleming H. Revell, 1951.

Fiske, John. "The Meaning of Infancy" (1871). *Excursions of an Evolutionist*. London: Macmillan, 1884, pp. 306-336.

Freedman, Seymour E. *The Book of Kashruth: A Treasury of Kosher Facts*. New York: Bloch, 1970.

Freud, Sigmund. *Civilization and Its Discontents*. London: Hogarth, 1955.

──────. *The Future of an Illusion*. Garden City: Anchor Books, 1964.

──────. "Obsessive Acts and Religious Practices."In *Collected Papers*, vol. 2, pp. 25-35.

Friedman, Sol Bezalel. "Kashruth and Civil Kosher Law Enforcement in the United States, Canada, South America, Parts of the British Empire, and Israel." Ph.D. diss., Yeshiva University, 1961.

Giehl, Dudley, *Vegetarianism: A Way of Life*. New York: Harper & Row, 1979.

Ginzberg, Louis. *Legends of the Bible*. Philadelphia, Jewish Publication Society, 1956.

Gordon, Hirsch Loeb. "Hygiene of the Jews." In *Universal Jewish Encyclopedia*. New York: Ktav, 1961.

Green, Joe. *The Jewish Vegetarian Tradition*. Mimeographed. Johannesburg, 1969, published by the author.

Greenstone, Julius H. "Health Laws." In *Jewish Encyclopedia*. New York: Funk & Wagnalls, 1904.

Grollman, Earl A. *Judaism in Sigmund Freud's World*. New York: Appleton-Century, 1965.

Groner, Arlene Pianko. "The Greening of Kashrut." *National Jewish Monthly*, April 1976, pp. 12-20.

Hagler, Louise (ed.) *The Farm Vegetarian Cookbook*. Rev. ed. Summertown, Tenn.: Book Publishing Co., 1978.

Harris, Maurice H. *A Thousand Years of Jewish History*. New York: Bloch, 1923.

Herdt, Sheryll P. *Nitty Gritty Foodbook*. New York: Praeger, 1975.

Hertz, J. H. (ed.) *The Pentateuch and Haftorahs*. 2d ed. London: Soncino Press, 1965.

Hogg, G. "Cannibalism and Human Sacrifice." *Encyclopaedia Britannica*, Chicago, 1966.

Howell, F. Clark, et al. *Early Man*. New York: Time-Life Books, 1965.

Isaac, Erich. "Forbidden Foods." *Commentary*, January 1966, pp. 36-41.

Jacobs, Louis. *What Does Judaism Say About . . . ?* New York: Quadrangle, 1973.

Jameson, R. D. "Cannibalism." In *Funk and Wagnall's Standard Dictionary of Folklore, Mythology and Legend*, edited by Maria Leach. New York: Funk and Wagnalls, 1972.

Kaplan, Mordecai M. *Questions Jews Ask: Reconstructionist Answers.* New York: Reconstructionist Press, 1956.

Khrushchev, Nikita. *Khrushchev Remembers.* Boston: Little, Brown, 1970.

Kook, Abraham Isaac. "Hazon Ha'tzimhoniut V'hasholom" ("A Vision of Vegetarianism and Peace"). Combines two essays: "Afikim Banegev" ("Streams in the Desert"), 1903, and "Tallelei Orot" ("Dew Drops of Light"), 1914. Copy of combined essay obtained from Yeshiva University Library.

————. "Fragments of Light: A View as to the Reasons for the Commandments." In *Abraham Isaac Kook*, translated and introduced by Ben Zion Bokser, pp. 303-323. New York: Paulist Press, 1978.

Koppel, Gene, and Henry Kaufman. "Elie Wiesel: A Small Measure of Victory" [an interview]. Tucson: University of Arizona, 1974.

LaBarre, Weston. *The Human Animal.* Chicago: University of Chicago Press, 1954.

Lappé, Frances Moore. *Diet for a Small Planet.* Rev. ed. New York: Friends of the Earth/Ballantine, 1975.

Leftwich, Joseph. Foreword to *Tree of Life*, edited by Philip L. Pick. New York: A. S. Barnes, 1977.

Levi, Leo. *Vistas from Mount Moriah. A Scientist Views Judaism and the World.* New York: Gur Publishing Co., 1959.

Levin, S. I., and Edward A. Boyden. *Kosher Code of the Orthodox Jew.* New York: Hermon Press, 1940.

Levy, Jacob. "Hygiene, Jewish." *Vallentine's Jewish Encyclopedia.* London: Shapiro, Vallentine, 1938.

Liebman, Charles S. "Orthodoxy in American Life," *American Jewish Year Book*, vol. 66, 1965, pp. 21-97.

Maimonides, Moses. *Mishneh Torah* [Code of Law and Ethics] translated and abridged by Philip Birnbaum. New York: Hebrew Publishing Co., 1944.

————. *Guide for the Perplexed.* Friedlander translation.

Matt, Hershel. "Kashrut in Conservative Judaism," *Conservative Judaism*, Fall 1957, vol. 12, no. 1, pages 34-38.

Mayer, Jean. "Amino Acid Requirements of Man." In the author's *Human Nutrition: Its Physiological, Medical and Social Aspects*. Springfield, Ill.: Charles C. Thomas, 1972.

Milgrom, Joseph. "Leviticus, Book of." *Encyclopaedia Judaica* (1972), vol. 11, cols. 138-147.

Neher, André, and Yaacov Mazor. "Hasidism." *Encyclopaedia Judaica* (1972), vol. 7. cols. 1390-1427.

Preuss, Julius. *Biblisch-Talmudische Medizin.* Berlin: Karger, 1923. In English: *Julius Preuss' "Biblical and Talmudic Medicine,"* translated by Fred Rosner. New York: Sanhedrin Press, 1978.

Rabinowitz, Louis I. "Rabbinics v. Vegetarianism?" *Jewish Vegetarian*, no. 45 (Summer 1978), pages 34-35.

Reik, Theodor. *Dogma and Compulsion.* New York: International Universities Press. 1951.

――――. *Mystery on the Mountain: The Drama of the Sinai Revelation.* New York: Harper, 1959.

Robertson, Laurel, et al. *Laurel's Kitchen: A Handbook for Vegetarian Cookery and Nutrition.* Petaluma, Calif.: Nilgri Press, 1976. (Available in Bantam paperback.)

Rose, W. C. "The Amino Acid Requirements of Man." *Federal Proceedings of American Societies for Experimental Biology*, vol. 8, (1949), p. 546.

Rosenberg, Stuart E. *America Is Different.* New York: Thomas Nelson & Sons, 1964.

Rubenstein, Richard. "The Making of a Rabbi." In *The Religious Personality*, edited by Donald and Walter Capps, pp. 254-266. Belmont, Calif.: Wadsworth, 1970.

Shapiro, Solomon S. "The Humaneness of Schechita." In *Essays, Timely and Timeless*, by the author. Published by the author, New York, 1961.

Shenker, Israel. *Noshing Is Sacred.* Indianapolis: Bobbs-Merrill Co., 1979.

Shulchan Aruch. See Caro, Joseph.

Silberman, Lou Hackett. "Judaism." *Encyclopaedia Britannica*, 15th ed. Chicago, 1975.

Simoons, Frederick J. *Eat Not This Flesh: Food Avoidances in the Old World.* Madison: University of Wisconsin Press, 1961.

Singer, Isaac Bashevis. *The Manor.* New York: Farrar, Straus & Giroux, 1967.

Soler, Jean. "The Dietary Prohibitions of the Hebrews." *New York Review of Books*, 23:10 (June 14, 1979), pp. 24-30.

Soncino Pentatench. *See* Hertz, J. H.

Stefansson, Vilhjamur. *Not by Bread Alone.* New York: Macmillan: 1946.

Sussman, Vic. *The Vegetarian Alternative.* Emmaus, Pa.: Rodale Press, 1978.

Tannahill, Reay. *Flesh and Blood: A History of the Cannibal Complex.* New York: Stein & Day, 1975.

――――. *Food in History.* New York: Stein & Day, 1973.

van den Haag, Ernest. *Passion and Social Constraint.* New York: Stein & Day, 1963.

Williams, Roger J. *Biochemical Individuality.* New York: Wiley, 1956.

――――. *Nutrition in a Nutshell.* Garden City, N.Y.: Doubleday Dolphin Books, 1962.

Wisse, Ruth R. "Singer's Paradoxical Progress," *Commentary*, February 1979, pp. 33-38.

GENERAL INDEX

INDEX TO BIBLICAL REFERENCES

NUTRITION AND COOKERY INDEX